M000210077

Arabic
Conversation Book

Mohd. Harun Rashid
Khalid Perwez

GOODWORD BOOKS

First Published 2004
Reprinted 2006

Goodword Books Pvt. Ltd.
1, Nizamuddin West Market
New Delhi-110 013
e-mail: info@goodwordbooks.com
Printed in India

www.goodwordbooks.com

Preface

Arabic is one of the most widely spoken languages in the world. With the economic development and prosperity in the Arab world the importance of Arabic has considerably increased.

This *Arabic Conversation Book* is an invaluable guide to modem spoken Arabic. It has been specially designed for tourists, business travelers and students who wish to acquire a certain amount of proficiency in spoken Arabic in a short span of time. The book is aimed at imparting basic communicative skills in spoken Arabic. Therefore, all efforts have been made to represent words and expressions which are simple and easy. This book is intended to serve the need of those whose aim is to speak Arabic fluently and confidently in a short time. The book covers a wide range of topics from airport to hotel, from eating to clothing, from restaurant to shopping and many more.

Throughout the book it has been our effort to present the important phrases and words that a common man and in particular a tourist or a business traveler often needs to know in order to speak effortlessly during his or her visit to an Arab country. All expressions in the book have been given in modem standard Arabic. To help those who can't read Arabic, we have especially transcribed the Arabic text into English.

We believe this Arabic phrase book will provide the learners with basic and working knowledge of the Arabic language and enable them to understand and communicate Arabic in an excellent manner.

M. Harun Rashid
September 2004

Contents

(al-muḥtawayāt) المحتويات

Introduction

(atta'āruf) التَّعَارُف

Jamal: Good morning.	*Jamāl: ṣabāḥal khair*	جَمَال: صَبَاحَ الْخَيْر
Nasir: Good morning. How are you?	*Nāṣir: ṣabāḥan nūr kaifa ḥāluk?*	نَاصِر: صَبَاحَ النُّور، كَيْفَ حَالُك؟
Jamal: I am fine, thank you. And how are you?	*Jamāl: anā bikhair, shukran, wa kaifa ḥāluk?*	جَمَال: أَنَا بِخَيْر، شُكْراً، وَكَيْفَ حَالُك؟
Nasir: I am very well, thank you.	*Nāṣir: anā bikhair wa 'āfiah, shukran.*	نَاصِر: أَنَا بِخَيْر وَعَافِيَة، شُكْراً
Jamal: What is your name?	*Jamāl: masmuk?*	جَمَال: مَا اسْمُك؟
Nasir: My name is Nasir. And what is your name?	*Nāṣir: ismī Nāṣir. wasmuk?*	نَاصِر: اِسْمِي نَاصِر. وَاسْمُك؟
Jamal: My name is Jamal. Which country are you from?	*Jamāl: ismī Jamāl. min ayyi balad anta?*	جَمَال: اسْمِي جَمَال. مِنْ أَيِّ بَلَد أَنْتَ؟

Nasir: I am from England. And you?	*Nasīr: anā min injiltarā. wa anta?*	نَاصِر: أَنَا مِنْ إِنْجِلْتَرا. وأَنْتَ؟
Jamal: I am from New York.	*Jamāl: anā min new york.*	جَمَال: أَنَا مِنْ نيويُورك.
Nasir: What do you do in New York?	*Nāṣir: wa mādhā ta'mal fi new york?*	نَاصِر: وَمَاذَا تَعْمَل فِي نيويُورك؟
Jamal: I am a merchant. What about you?	*Jamāl: anā tājir. wa mā shughluk?*	جَمَال: أَنَا تَاجِر. وَمَا شُغْلُك؟
Nasir: I am a teacher by profession. I teach in Oxford University, England. I teach History and religion.	*Nāṣir: anā ashtaghilu mudarrisan, udarris fi jāmi'ati oxford, injiltra. udarrisut tārīkh wal adyān.*	نَاصِر: أَنَا أَشْتَغِلُ مُدَرِّسًا، أُدَرِّسُ فِي جَامِعَة آكْسفُورد، إِنْجلْترا. أُدَرِّسُ التَّارِيْخَ وَالأَدْيَان.
Jamal: Who is this lady with you?	*Jamāl: wa man hādhihis sayyidah ma'ak?*	جَمَال: وَمَنْ هَذه السَّيِّدَة مَعَك؟
Nasir: She is my wife, Zainab.	*Nāṣir: hiya zaujatī zainab.*	نَاصِر: هِيَ زَوْجَتِي زَيْنَب.
Jamal: Is she also a teacher?	*Jamāl: 'a hiya mudarrisah aiḍā?*	جَمَال: أَهِيَ مُدَرِّسَة أَيْضًا؟
Nasir: Yes, she teaches in a primary school in London.	*Nāṣir: na'am hiya tudarris fi madrasah ibtidā'iyyah fi landan.*	نَاصِر: نَعَم، هِيَ تُدَرِّسُ فِي مَدْرَسَة اِبْتِدَائِيَّة فِي لَنْدَن.
Nasir: Hello!	*Nāṣir: marḥabā*	نَاصِر: مَرْحَبًا
Zainab: Hello!	*Zainab: marḥabā*	زَيْنَب: مَرْحَبًا
Jamal: Who is this young man with you?	*Jamāl: wa man hādhash shābb ma'ak?*	جمال: وَمَنْ هَذَا الشَّابّ مَعَك؟
Nasir: He is my son Asad. He studies Engineering in Oxford University.	*Nāṣir: hādha ibnī As'ad, huwa yadrus al handasah fi jāmi'ati oxford.*	نَاصِر: هَذَا ابْنِي أَسْعَد، هُوَ يَدْرُسُ الْهَنْدَسَة فِي جَامِعَة آكسفورد.

Where do you live in New York?	*aina taskun fī newyork ?*	أَيْنَ تَسْكُنُ فِي نيويُورك؟
Jamal: I live in Valley Streame.	*Jamāl: askun fī walī istrīm.*	جَمَال: أَسْكُن فِي وِيلي اسْتريم.
When did you arrive in Cairo?	*matā waṣalta ilal qāhirah?*	مَتَى وَصَلْتَ إلَى الْقَاهِرَة؟
Nasir: Last week.	*Nāṣir: al usbū' al māḍī.*	نَاصِر: الأسْبُوعَ الْمَاضِي.
Jamal:What do you plan to do here?	*Jamāl: wa mā taqṣid hunā?*	جَمَال: وَمَا تَقْصِد هُنَا؟
Nasir: We plan to visit the Egyptian Museum and other historical places. And what about you?	*Nāṣir: urīd an azūr al matḥaf al miṣriyy wal amākin at tārīkhiyyah al ukhrā. wa anta?*	نَاصِر: أُرِيْدُ أَنْ أَزُوْرَ الْمَتْحَفَ الْمصْرِي وَالأمَاكِنَ التَّارِيْخِيَّة الأُخْرَى. وَأَنْتَ؟
Jamal:I have to attend to some important work here.	*Jamāl: qad ji'tu hunā li ba'ḍ shu'ūn hāmmah.*	جَمَال: قَدْ جِئْتُ هُنَا لِبَعْض شُئُونٍ هَامَّةٍ.
Nasir: When will you return to New York?	*Nāṣir: matā tarji' ilā newyork?*	نَاصِر: مَتَى تَرْجِع إِلَى نيويُورك؟
Jamal: After a week.	*Jamāl: ba'da usbū'.*	جَمَال: بَعْدَ أُسْبُوع.
Jamal: I feel like having something. Would you also like to have anything, sir?	*Jamāl: urīd an ākhudh shay'ā. hal tawadd an ta'khudh shay'an aiḍan sayyidī?*	جَمَال:أُرِيْدُ أَنْ آخُذَ شَيْئًا. هَلْ تَوَدّ أَنْ تَأْخُذَ شَيْئًا أَيْضاً سَيِّدِي؟
Nasir: Yes, I would like to have coffee.	*Nāṣir: na'am 'awadd an ākhudh al qahwah.*	نَاصِر: نَعَم، أَوَدّ أَنْ آخُذَ القَهْوَة.
Jamal: Good. Let us go to the cafeteria and take coffeee.	*Jamāl: ḥasanan, hayyā bina nadhhab ilal maqhā wa nashrabil qahwah.*	جمال: حَسَنًا، هَيَّا بِنَا نَذْهَبُ إِلَى الْمَقْهَى وَنَشْرَبِ الْقَهْوَة.
Can you please give me your address and	*hal tu'ṭīnī 'unwānak wa raqma hātifik*	هَلْ تُعْطِيْنِي عُنْوَانَك وَرَقْمَ [illegible]

telephone no?	*min faḍlik?*	هَاتفك منْ فَضْلك؟
Nasir: Yes, why not? Here is my address and telephone number.	*Nāṣir: na'am, walima lā, hādhā 'unwānī wa hādhā raqmul hātif.*	نَاصر: نَعَم، وَلِمَ لاَ؟ هَذَا عُنْوَانِي وَهَذَا رَقْمُ الْهَاتِف.
Jamal: Thank you very much.	*Jamāl: shukran jazīlā.*	جَمَال: شُكْراً جَزِيْلاً.
Nasir: Can I have yours?	*Nāṣir: hal yumkin an ākhudh 'unwānak aiḍan?*	نَاصر: هَلْ يُمْكِن أنْ آخُذَ عُنْوَانَك أيْضاً؟
Jamal: Oh yes, why not? Here it is.	*Jamāl: ay na'am, wa lima la? wa hā huwa dhā*	جَمَال: أيْ نَعَم، وَلِمَ لاَ؟ وَهَا هُوَ ذَا.
I will write to you after I get back to New York.	*anā aktub ilaika ba'da wuṣūlī ilā newyork.*	أنَا أكْتُب إلَيْكَ بَعْدَ وُصُولِي إلَى نِيويُورك.
Nasir: Thank you. Goodbye	*Nāṣir: shukran, ma'as salāmah.*	نَاصر: شُكْراً، مَعَ السَّلاَمَة.
Jamal: Goodbye	*Jamāl: ma'as salāmah ilal liqā'.*	جَمَال: مَعَ السَّلاَمَة إلَى اللّقَاء

At the Airport

(fil maṭār) فِي الْمَطَار

Jamal is a businessman from New York.	*Jamāl rajulu a'māl min newyork.*	جَمَال رَجُلُ أَعْمَالٍ مِنْ نيويُورك.
He takes a flight from New York to Cairo, Egypt.	*huwa ya'khudh aṭ ṭā'irah min newyork ilal qāhirah, miṣr.*	هُوَ يَأخُذُ الطَّائِرَةَ مِن نِيويُورك إلَى الْقَاهِرَة، مِصْر.
After arrving at Cairo Airport he collects his luggage and goes to the immigration officer.	*ba'dal wuṣūl ilā maṭāril qāhirah ya'khudh 'afashah wa yatawajjah ilā shubbākil jawāzāt.*	بَعْدَ الْوُصُول إلَى مَطَارِ الْقَاهِرَة يَأخُذ عَفَشَه وَيَتَوَجَّه إلَى شُبَّاك الْجَوَازَات.
The following convers-ation takes place betw-een the immigration officer and him.	*wayajrī bainahumā al hadīth al ātī.*	وَيَجْرِي بَيْنَهُمَا الْحَدِيْثُ الآتِي
Immigration officer: Which country are you from, sir?	*ḍābiṭul jawāzāt: min ayyi balad anta yā sayyidī?*	ضَابِطُ الْجَوَازَات: مِنْ أَيِّ بَلَد أَنْتَ يَا سَيِّدِي؟
Jamal: America.	*Jamāl: min amrīkā.*	جَمَال: مِنْ أَمْرِيكا.
Officer: May I know your name, sir?	*ḍābiṭ: man ḥaḍratuk min faḍlik?*	ضَابِط: مَنْ حَضرَتُك مِن فَضْلِك؟

Jamal: My name is Jamal.	*Jamāl: ismī jamāl.*	جَمَال: اِسْمِي جَمَال.
Officer: can you show me your passport, sir?	*ḍābiṭ: hal turīnī jawāza safarik yā sayyidī?*	ضَابِط: هَلْ تُرِيْنِي جَوَازَ سَفَرِك يَا سَيِّدِي؟
Jamal: Yes. This is my passport.	*Jamāl: hādhā huwa jawāzu safarī.*	جَمَال: هَذَا هُوَ جَوَازُ سَفَرِي.
Officer: Have you filled in your arrival card?	*ḍābiṭ: hal mala'ta biṭāqatal wuṣūl?*	ضَابِط: هَلْ مَلَأْتَ بِطَاقَةَ الْوُصُول؟
Jamal: Yes, here it is.	*Jamāl: na'am, hādhihi hiyal biṭāqah..*	جَمَال: نَعَم، هَذِه هِيَ الْبِطَاقَة.
Custom Officer: Have you got any foreign goods with you, sir?	*mufattishul jumruk: hal 'indak baḍā'i' ajnabiyyah yā sayyidī?*	مُفَتِّشُ الْجُمْرُك: هَلْ عِنْدَك بَضَائِع أَجْنَبِيَّة يَا سَيِّدِي؟
Jamal: Yes, I have got a computer and a Japanese watch.	*Jamāl: na'am 'indī kambiutar wa sā'ah yābāniyyah.*	جَمَال: نَعَم، عِنْدِي كَمْبِيوتَر وَسَاعَة يَابَانِيَّة.
Officer: What is there in this big box?	*mufattish: wa mā fī hādhaṣ ṣundūq al kabīr?*	مُفَتِّش: وَمَا فِي هَذَا الصُّنْدُوق الْكَبِير؟
Jamal: There are some books in it.	*Jamāl: fīhi ba'ḍul kutub.*	جَمَال: فِيه بَعْضُ الْكُتُب.
Officer: Any other goods to declare?	*mufattish: shay' ākhar lit taṣrīh̲.*	مُفَتِّش: شَيْء آخَر لِلتَّصْرِيْح؟
Jamal: No, nothing more.	*Jamāl: lā, lā shay' ākhar.*	جَمَال: لاَ، لاَ شَيْء آخَر.
Officer: Could you please weigh this box?	*mufattish: hal tazin hādhaṣ ṣundūq min faḍlik?*	مُفَتِّش: هَلْ تَزِنُ هَذَا الصُّنْدُوق مِنْ فَضْلك؟
Jamal: Oh! Sure.	*Jamāl: ay na'am.*	جَمَال: أَيْ نَعَم.
Any other formalities?	*ayya ijrā'āt ukhrā ?*	أَيَّ إِجْرَاءَات أُخْرَى؟
Officer: No, sir.	*mufattish: lā, yā sayyidī.*	مُفَتِّش: لاَ، يَا سَيِّدِي؟
Jamal: Thank you.	*Jamāl: shukran.*	جَمَال: شُكْراً.
Officer: Not at all.	*Mufattish: 'afwā.*	مُفَتِّش: عَفْوًا.

From the arrival hall Jamal goes to the waiting hall. His friend faisal meets him there:	*yatawajjah Jamāl min ṣālatil wuṣūl ilā ṣālatil intiẓār yuqābiluhu ṣadīquhu Faiṣal hunāk.*	يَتَوَجَّهُ جَمَال مِنْ صَالَة الْوُصُول إِلَى صَالَة الانْتِظَار. يُقَابِلُه صَدِيْقُهُ فَيصَل هُنَاك:
Faisal: Welcome, friend. How are you?	*Faiṣal: ahlan wa sahlan wa marḥabam bik. kaifal ḥāl yā ṣadīqī ?*	فَيصَل: أهلاً وَسَهْلاً وَمَرْحَباً بك. كَيْفَ الْحَال يَا صَدِيْقِي؟
Jamal: Fine. And you?	*Jamāl: ṭayyib, wa anta?*	جَمَال: طَيِّب، وَأَنْتَ؟
Faisal: I am very well. Thank you.	*Faiṣal: anā bikhair wa 'āfiah, shukran.*	فَيصَل: أَنَا بِخَيْر وَعَافِيَة، شُكْراً.
What time did you leave New York, friend?	*matā ghādarta newyork yā ṣadīqī?*	مَتَى غَادَرْتَ نيويُورك يَا صَدِيْقِي؟
Jamal: At ten in the morning.	*Jamāl: fis sā'atil 'āshira ṣabāḥan.*	جَمَال: فِي السَّاعَة الْعَاشِرَة صَبَاحًا.
Faisal: How was the journey?	*Faisal: kaifa kānas safar?*	فَيصَل: كَيْفَ كَانَ السَّفَر؟
Jamal: It was very comfortable.	*Jamāl: innahu kāna murīḥan jiddā.*	جَمَال: إِنَّه كَان مُرِيْحاً جِدًّا.
Journeys are very comfortable these days.	*al asfāru murīḥatun jiddā fī hādhihil ayyām.*	الأسفَارُ مُرِيْحَةٌ جِدًّا فِي هَذِه الأيَّام.
Faisal: Where would you like to stay?	*Faiṣal: aina tuḥibb an tuqīm yā ṣadīqī ?*	فَيصَل: أَيْنَ تُحِبُّ أَنْ تُقِيْمَ يَا صَدِيْقِي؟
Jamal: In a good, clean hotel.	*Jamāl: fī funduq jayyid wa naẓīf.*	جَمَال: فِي فُنْدُق جَيِّد و نَظِيْف.
Faisal: Then lets go to Hilton Hotel which is located in the heart of Cairo.	*Faiṣal: falnadhhab ilā funduq hilton al wāqi' fī qalbil qāhirah.*	فَيصَل: فَلْنَذْهَبْ إِلَى فُنْدُق هلتُون الوَاقِع فِي قَلْب الْقَاهِرَة.
Jamal and Faisal come out of the waiting hall and go to the taxi stand. The following conversation takes	*Jamāl wa Faiṣal yakhrujān min ṣālatil intiẓār wa yadhhabān ilā mawqifis sayyārāt wa yadūr bainahumā wa baina sā'iqit tāksī*	جَمَال وَ فَيصَل يَخْرُجَان مِنْ صَالَة الانْتِظَار وَيَذْهَبَان إِلَى مَوْقِف السَّيَّارَات وَيَدُور بَيْنَهُمَا وَ بَيْنَ سَائِق التَّاكْسِي

place between them and the taxi driver.	*hādhal ḥiwār:*	هَذَا الْحِوَار:
Taxi driver: Welcome sir!	*sā'iqut tāksī: marḥabam bikum yā sayyidī.*	سَائِق التَّاكْسِي: مَرْحَباً بِكُم يَا سَيِّدِي.
Where do you want to go?	*aina turīd an tadhhab?*	أَيْنَ تُرِيْدُ أَنْ تَذْهَب؟
Jamal: We want to go to Hilton Hotel.	*Jamāl: nurīdudh dhahāb ilā funduq hilton.*	جَمَال:نُرِيْدُ الذَّهَابَ إِلَى فُنْدُق هِلْتُون.
Driver: Are you a tourist, sir?	*assāiq: hal anta sayyāḥ yā sayyidī?*	السَّائِق: هَلْ أَنْتَ سَيَّاح يَا سَيِّدِي؟
Jamal: yes, I am a business tourist. I have come here from New York for an important work.	*Jamāl: na'am anā sayyāḥ tijāriyy. qad ji'tu hunā min newyork li shughl muhimm.*	جَمَال: نَعَم، أنَا سَيَّاح تِجَارِي. قَدْ جِئْتُ هُنَا مِنْ نِيويُورك لِشُغْلٍ مُهِمّ.
Fasal: What is the fare for Hilton Hotel?	*Faiṣal: mā hiyal ujrah ilā funduq Hilton ?*	فَيصَل: مَا هِيَ الأُجْرَة إِلَى فُنْدُق هِلْتُون؟
Driver: Thirty Egyptian pounds.	*assā'iq: thalāthūna junaihan miṣriyyā.*	السَّائِق: ثَلاثُون جُنَيْهًا مِصْرِيًّا.
Jamal: How far is Hilton Hotel from here?	*Jamāl: kam yab'ud funduq hilton min hunā?*	جَمَال: كَمْ يَبْعُد فُنْدُق هِلْتُون مِنْ هُنَا؟
Driver: Fifty k.m. from here.	*assā'iq: khamsīna kilo mitran min hunā.*	السَّائِق: خَمْسِيْنَ كِيْلُو مِترًا مِنْ هُنَا.
Jamal: How many hours will it take to reach the hotel?	*Jamāl: kam sā'ah yastaghriq al wuṣūl ilal funduq?*	جَمَال:كَمْ سَاعَةً يَسْتَغْرِقُ الْوُصُول إِلَى الْفُنْدُق؟
Driver: It will take only an hour.	*assā'iq: yastaghriq sā'ah wāḥidah faqat.*	السَّائِق: يَسْتَغْرِق سَاعَةً وَاحِدَة فَقَط.
After arriving at the hotel Jamal pays the fare to the driver and both Faisal and Jamal enter the hotel.	*ba'dal wuṣūl ilal funduq Jamāl yadfa'ul ujrah ilas sā'iq wa kilāhumā yadkhulānil funduq.*	بَعْدَ الْوُصُول إِلَى الْفُنْدُق جَمَال يَدفَعُ الأُجْرَة إِلَى السَّائِق وَكِلاهُمَا يَدْخُلاَن الْفُنْدُق.

In the Hotel

(fil funduq) فِي الْفُنْدُق

Receptionist: Welcome sir! What can I do for you?	*muwazzaful istiqbāl: ahlan wa sahlan yā sayyidī ayya khidmah?*	مُوَظَّفُ الاسْتِقْبَال: أَهْلاً وَسَهْلاً يَا سَيِّدِيْ أيّ خِدْمَة؟
Jamal: I want to get a room for myself.	*Jamāl: urīd an aḥjuz lī ghurfah.*	جَمَال: أُرِيْدُ أَنْ أحْجُزَ لِي غُرفَة.
Receptionist: Are you alone?	*al muwazzaf: hal anta bi mufradik?*	المُوَظَّف: هَلْ أنْتَ بِمُفْرَدِك؟
Jamal: Yes.	*Jamāl: na'am.*	جَمَال: نَعَم.
Receptionist: What sort of room do you want?	*al muwazzaf: ayya nau' minal ghurfah turīd?*	الْمُوَظَّف: أيّ نَوْع مِنَ الْغُرْفَة تُرِيْد؟
Jamal: I want a single-bed room with attached bathroom.	*Jamāl: anā urīd ghurfah ma'a sarīr wa bi ḥammām khāṣṣ.*	جَمَال: أنَا أُرِيْد غُرْفَة مَعَ سَرِيْر وَ بِحَمَّام خَاصّ.
Receptionist: Every room in this hotel has an attached bathroom, sir.	*al muwazzaf: likulli ghurfah fi hādhal funduq ḥammām khāṣṣ yā sayyidī.*	المُوَظَّف: لِكُلِّ غُرْفَة فِي هَذَا الْفُنْدُق حَمَّام خَاصّ يَا سَيِّدِي.

Jamal: Is there a geyser also with bathroom for hot water?	*Jamāl: hal hunāk musakhkhin fil ḥammām?*	جَمَال: هَلْ هُنَاكَ مُسَخِّن فِي الْحَمَّام؟
Receptionist: Yes, every bathroom has a geyser.	*al muwaẓẓaf: na'am, likulli ḥammām musakhkhin.*	الْمُوَظَّف: نَعَم، لِكُلِّ حَمَّام مُسَخِّن.
Jamal: Is there a telephone also in the room?	*Jamāl: hal yūjad fīhā telifon aiḍā ?*	جَمَال: هَلْ يُوجَد فِيهَا تليفُون أَيْضًا؟
Receptionist: Sorry sir, this facility is not available.	*al muwaẓẓaf: āsif yā sayyidī, lā tatawaffar hādhihis suhūlah.*	الْمُوَظَّف: آسف يَا سَيِّدي، لاَ تَتَوَفَّر هَذِهِ السُّهُولَة.
Jamal: And television?	*Jamāl: wat tilfizyūn?*	جمال: وَالتِّلْفِزْيُون؟
Receptionist: Yes.	*al muwaẓẓaf: na'am.*	الموظَّف: نَعَم.
Jamal: What are the other facilities in the hotel?	*Jamāl: wa mā hiya tashīlāt ukhrā fil funduq ?*	جمال: وَمَاهِيَ تَسْهِيْلاتٌ أُخرَى فِي الْفُنْدُق؟
Receptionist: There is a restaurant, and a cafeteria in the hotel. You can get all kinds of eatables and drinkables there.	*al muwaẓẓaf: fīhi maṭ'am wa maqhā, tajid hunāk kulla naw' minal ma'kūlāt wal mashrūbāt.*	الْمُوَظَّف: فِيْه مَطْعَم وَمَقْهَى، تَجد هُنَاكَ كُلَّ نَوعٍ مِنَ الْمَأْكُولاَت وَالْمَشْرُوبَات.
Jamal: What is the charge for a day?	*Jamāl: mā hiyal ujrah li yawm?*	جَمَال: مَا هِيَ الأُجْرَة لِيَومٍ؟
Receptionist: Fifty dollars. How long are you going to stay?	*al muwaẓẓaf: khamsūna junaihā. likam muddah turīdul iqāmah?*	الْمُوَظَّف: خَمْسُونَ جُنَيْهاً. لِكَم مُدَّة تُرِيْدُ الإقَامَة؟
Jamal: For a week.	*Jamāl: li 'usbū'*	جَمَال: لأُسْبُوع.
Receptionist : Which floor do you want?	*al muwaẓẓaf: fī ayyi dawr turīd an tuqīm?*	الْمُوَظَّف: فِي أَيِّ دَوْر تُرِيْد أَنْ تُقِيْم؟
Jamal: Ground floor.	*Jamāl: fid dauril arḍī.*	جَمَال: فِي الدَّوْرِ الأَرْضِي.
Receptionist: Sorry sir, all the rooms on	*al muwaẓẓaf: āsif, yā sayyidī kullul ghuraf*	الْمُوَظَّف: آسف، يَا سَيِّدي

the ground floor are reserved.	*fid dauril arḍī mahjūzah.*	كُلُّ الْغُرَف فِي الدَّوْرِ الأَرْضِي مَحْجُوزَة.
Jamal: OK then, on the first floor?	*Jamāl: fa fid dauril awwal?*	جَمَال: حَسَنًا، فَفِي الدَّوْرِ الأَوَّل؟
Receptionist: Yes, sir. You can get a room in the first floor.	*al muwaẓẓaf: na'am yā sayyidī. yumkin an tajid ghurfah fid dauril awwal.*	المُوَظَّف: نَعَم، يَا سَيِّدي. يُمْكِنُ أَنْ تَجِد غُرْفَة فِي الدَّوْرِ الأَوَّل.
What is your name?	*masmuk?*	مَا اسْمُك؟
Jamal: My name is Jamal.	*Jamāl: ismī jamāl.*	جَمَال: اِسْمِي جَمَال.
Receptionist: And your address sir?	*al muwaẓẓaf: wa 'unwānuk yā sayyidī?*	المُوَظَّف: وَعُنْوَانُك يَا سَيِّدِي؟
Jamal: House No. 28, Columbus Street, New York.	*Jamāl: raqmu manzilī thamāniw wa 'ishrūn, shāri' kolambas, new york.*	جمال: رَقَمُ مَنْــزِلي ٢٨، شَارِع كُولَمْبَس، نِيويُورك.
Receptionist: What is the purpose of your visit?	*al muwaẓẓaf: mā sababu ziyāratik?*	المُوَظَّف: مَا سَبَبُ زِيَارَتك؟
Jamal: Business.	*Jamāl: at tijārah.*	جَمَال: التِّجَارَة.
Receptionist: Can you show me your passport? I have to note down its number.	*al muwaẓẓaf: hal turīnī jawāza safarik? urīd tasjīla raqmihi.*	الْمُوَظَّف: هَلْ تُرِيْنِي جَوَازَ سَفَرِك؟ أُرِيْدُ تَسْجِيْل رَقْمِه.
Jamal: Here is my passport. The number is 751690	*Jamāl: hādhā huwa jawāzu safarī. raqmuhu 751690*	جَمَال: هَذَا هُوَ جَوَازُ سَفَرِي. رَقْمُه ٧٥١٦٩٠
Receptionist: Your room number is 121 on the first floor and here is the key.	*al muwaẓẓaf: raqmu ghurfatik wāhiduw wa 'ishrūn wa mi'ah fid dauril awwal wa hādhā huwa miftāḥul ghurfah.*	الْمُوَظَّف: رَقَمُ غُرْفَتك ١٢١ فِي الدَّوْرِ الأَوَّل وَهَذَا هُوَ مِفْتَاحُ الْغُرْفَة.
Jamal: Thank you very much.	*Jamāl: shukran jazīlā.*	جَمَال: شُكْراً جَزِيْلاً.

Receptionist: Not at all.	*al muwazzaf: 'afwā.*	الْمُوَظَّف: عفواً.
Receptionist calls a waiter to take the luggage of Jamal to his room.	*yad'ul muwazzaf nādilan liyaḥmila 'afasha Jamāl ilā ghurfatih.*	يَدْعُو الْمُوَظَّفُ نَادلاً لِيَحْمِلَ عفَشَ جَمَال إِلَى غُرْفَتِه.

In the Restaurant

(fil maṭ‘am) فى الْمَطْعَم

Jamal and Faisal go to the restaurant. All kinds of eatable and drinkable are served there.	*Jamal wa Faisal yadkhulānil maṭ‘am. yatawaffar fīhi kullu nau‘ minal ma’kūlāt wal mashrūbāt.*	جَمَال وَفَيصَل يَدْخُلاَن الْمَطْعَم. يَتوَفَّر فيْه كُلُّ نَوْعٍ مِنَ الْمَاكُولاَتِ وَالْمَشْرُوبَات.
The waiter welcomes them and the following conversation takes place between them.	*yuraḥḥibu bihimal jarsūn wa yajrī bainahum al ḥadīth al ātī.*	يُرَحِّبُ بِهِمَا الْجَرْسُون وَيَجْرِى بَيْنَهُمُ الْحَدِيْثُ الآتِي.
Waiter: Welcome sir! What would you like to have?	*al jarsūn: ahlan wa sahlan yā sayyidī. mādhā tawadd an ta’khudh?*	الْجَرْسُون: أَهْلاً وَسَهْلاً يَا سَيِّدِي. مَاذَا تَوَدُّ أَنْ تَأْخُذ؟
Jamal: First, I would like to see the menu?	*Jamāl: awwalan arinī qā’imatal ma’kūlāt ?*	جَمَال: أَوَّلاً أَرِنِي قَائِمَةَ الْمَأْكُولاَت؟
Waiter: Here is the menu sir.	*al jarsūn: hākal qā’imah yā sayyidī.*	الْجَرْسُون: هَاكَ الْقَائِمَة يَا سَيِّدِي.
Waiter: What would you prefer to have, sir?	*al jarsūn: māḍhā tufaḍḍil yā sayyidī ?*	الْجَرْسُون: مَاذَا تُفَضِّل يَا سَيِّدِي؟

Jamal: Have you got fried chicken?	*Jamāl: hal ʻindakum dajāj maqliyy?*	جَمَال: هَلْ عِنْدَكُم دَجَاج مَقْلِيّ؟
Waiter: Yes, sir. We have both fried and roasted chicken.	*al jarsūn: naʻam yā sayyidī. ʻindanā dajāj maqliyy wa dajāj bil furn aiḍā.*	الْجَرسُون: نَعَم، يَا سَيِّدي. عِنْدَنَا دَجَاج مَقْلِيّ وَ دَجَاج بِالْفُرْن أيْضًا.
Jamal: I'll take fried chicken. And what would you like to take, Faisal?	*Jamāl: anā ākhudh dajājan maqliyyā. wa mādhā tuḥibb an ta'khudh yā Faiṣal?*	جَمَال: أنَا آخُذُ دَجَاجًا مَقْلِيًّا. وَمَاذَا تُحِبُّ أن تَأخُذَ يَا فَيصَل؟
Faisal: I'll take roasted chicken.	*Faiṣal: anā ākhudh dajājan bil furn.*	فَيصَل: أنَا آخُذ دَجَاجًا بِالْفُرْن.
Jamal: OK, then, bring a plate of fried chicken and a plate of roasted chicken.	*Jamāl: ḥasanan, idhan hāti ṭabaqa dajāj maqliyy a ṭabaqa dajāj bil furn.*	جَمَال: حَسَنًا، إذَنْ هَات طَبَقَ دَجَاجِ مَقْلِيّ وَطَبَقَ دَجَاج بِالْفُرْن.
Waiter: Anything else, sir?	*al jarsūn: ayya shay' ākhar yā sayyidī?*	الْجَرسُون: أيَّ شَيْءٍ آخَر يَا سَيِّدي؟
Jamal: Yes, two plates of kabsah and some salad also.	*Jamāl: naʻam hāti ṭabaqain minal kabsah wa salṭah aiḍan.*	جَمَال: نَعَم، هَات طَبَقَيْن مِنَ الْكَبْسَة وَ سَلْطَة أيْضًا.
Waiter: Allright, sir.	*al jarsūn: naʻam ya sayyidī.*	الْجَرسُون: نَعَم، يَا سَيِّدي.
Faisal: Thank you.	*Faiṣal: shukran*	فَيصَل: شُكْراً
Waiter: Would you like to have dessert also?	*al jarsūn: hal tawadd an ta'khudh ḥalwā aiḍan?*	الْجَرسُون: هَلْ تَوَدُّ أنْ تَأخُذَ حَلْوَى أيْضًا؟
Faisal: Yes, what do you have for dessert?	*Faiṣal: naʻam, wa mādhā ʻindakum min ḥalwayāt.*	فَيصَل: نَعَم، وَمَاذَا عِنْدَكُم مِنْ حَلْوَيَات؟
Waiter: We have different varieties of pastries, fruit juice, vegetable juice, cake and ice-cream also.	*al jarsūn: ʻindanā faṭā'ir mukhtalifah, wa ʻaṣīr fawākih wa ʻaṣīr khaḍrāwāt, wa kaʻak wa būẓah aiḍan.*	الْجَرسُون: عِنْدَنَا فَطَائِر مُخْتَلِفَة، وَعَصِير فَوَاكِه، وَعَصِير خَضْرَاوَات، وَكَعْك وَبُوظَة أيْضاً.

Faisal: I'll take ice cream. And what would you like to take, jamal?	*Faiṣal: anā ākhudh būẓah. wa mādhā tuḥibb an ta'khudh yā Jamāl ?*	فَيصَل: أنَا آخُذُ بُوظَة. وَمَاذَا تُحِبُّ أَنْ تَأخُذَ يَا جَمَال؟
Jamal: I'll also take ice cream.	*Jamāl: anā aiḍan ākhudh ka'kah.*	جَمَال: أنَا أيضًا آخُذُ كَعْكَة.
Waiter: Any beverage, coffee or tea?	*al jarsūn: wa minal mashrūbāt qahwah am shāy?*	الْجَرْسُون: وَمِنَ الْمَشْرُوبَات، قَهْوَة أم شَاي؟
Jamal: I'll take coffee. And you Faisal?	*Jamāl: anā ākhudh qahwah. wa anta yā Faiṣal?*	جَمَال: أنَا آخُذُ قَهْوَة. وَأنْتَ يَا فَيصَل؟
Faisal: I'll have no coffee or tea.	*Faisal: lā qahwah wa lā shāy.*	فَيصَل: لاَ قَهْوَة وَلاَ شَاي.
Jamal: Please bring only a cup of coffee.	*Jamāl: īti bi finjān qahwah faqaṭ.*	جَمَال: ائْت بِفنْجَان قَهْوَة فَقَط.
Jamal: Could you please bring the bill?	*Jamāl: hāti al fātūrah min faḍlik ?*	جَمَال: هَات الْفَاتُورَة مِن فَضْلك؟
Waiter: Yes, sir. Here is the bill.	*al jarsūn: na'am, sayyidī. hādhihi hiyal fātūrah.*	الْجَرسُون: نَعَم، سَيِّدي هَذه هيَ الْفَاتُورَة.
Jamal: Thank you.	*Jamāl: shukran.*	جَمَال: شُكْراً.

In the Bank

(fil bank) فِي الْبَنْك

Jamal: Hello.	*Jamāl: marḥabā.*	جَمَال: مَرْحَبًا
Faisal: Hello.	*Faiṣal: marḥabā.*	فَيصَل: مَرْحَبًا
Jamal: O brother! Where are you going?	*Jamāl: aina tadhhab yā akhī ?*	جَمَال: أيْنَ تَذْهَب يَا أَخِي؟
Faisal: To the bank	*Faisal: ilal bank.*	فَيصَل: إلَى الْبَنْك.
Jamal: Any important work there?	*Jamāl: hal hunāk amr muhimm?*	جَمَال: هَلْ هُنَاكَ أمر مُهِمّ؟
Faisal: Yes, I have to open my bank account.	*Faiṣal: na'am urīd an aftaḥal ḥisāb fil bank.*	فَيصَل: نَعَم، أُرِيْد أن أفْتَحَ الْحِسَاب فِي الْبَنْك.
Jamal: Which bank are you going?	*Jamāl: ayya bank tadhhab?*	جَمَال: أيَّ بَنك تَذْهَب؟
Faisal: Central Bank.	*Faiṣal: al bank al markazī.*	فَيصَل: الْبَنْك الْمَرْكَزِيّ.
Jamal: Do you want to open account in your name or a joint account?	*Jamal: hal turīd an taftaḥal ḥisāb bismik amil ḥisāb al mushtarak?*	جَمَال: هَلْ تُرِيْد أنْ تَفْتَحَ الْحِسَاب بِاسْمِك أمِ الْحِسَابَ الْمُشْتَرَك؟

Faisal: Account in my name only. Would you accompany me?	*Faiṣal: ḥisāb bismī faqaṭ. hal tawadd an tuṣāḥibanī?*	فَيصَل: حسَاب باسْمِي فَقَط. هَلْ تَوَدُّ أَنْ تُصَاحِبَنِي؟
Jamal: Oh yes, brother! I'm also going to the bank. I have to withdraw some money from my account.	*Jamāl: na'am yā akhī. anā aiḍan adhhab ilal bank. urīd an asḥab ba'ḍan nuqūd min ḥisābī.*	جَمَال: نَعَم، يَا أَخِي. أَنَا أَيْضاً أَذْهَب إِلَى الْبَنْك. أُرِيْد أَنْ أَسْحَب بَعْضَ النُّقُود مِنْ حِسَابِي.
Faisal and Jamal both enter the bank and go straight to help desk.	*yadkhul Jamāl wa Faiṣal al bank wa yadhhabān ilā maktabil musā'adah.*	يَدْخُل جَمَال وَ فَيصَل الْبَنْك وَيَذْهَبَان إِلَى مَكْتَب الْمُسَاعَدَة.
Bank Employee: Good morning. May I help you?	*muwaẓẓaful bank: sabāḥal khair. ayya musā'adah?*	مُوَظَّفُ الْبَنْك: صَبَاحَ الْخَيْر. أَيَّ مُسَاعَدَة؟
Faisal: Yes, I want to open an account in my name. What do I need to do for this?	*Faiṣal: na'am urīd fatḥal ḥisāb bismī. mā hiyal ijrā'āt lidhālik?*	فَيصَل: نَعَم، أُرِيْد فَتْح الْحسَاب باسْمِي. مَا هِيَ الإجْرَاءَات لِذَلِك؟
Employee: You have to first fill the form. Have you got the form?	*al muwaẓẓaf: awwalan imla'il istimārah. hal 'indak istimārah?*	الْمُوَظَّف: أَوَّلاً امْلَأْ الاسْتِمَارَة. هَلْ عِنْدَك اسْتِمَارَة؟
Faisal: No, sir. Where will I get this form?	*Faiṣal: lā, yā sayyidī. wa min aina aḥṣul alaihā?*	فَيصَل: لاَ، يَا سَيِّدِي. وَمِن أَيْنَ أَحْصُل عَلَيْهَا؟
Employee: You have to go to counter no 5.	*al muwaẓẓaf: idhhab lidhālik ilā shubbāk raqm khamsah.*	الْمُوَظَّف: اذْهَب لِذَلِكَ إِلَى شُبَّاك رَقْم ٥
Faisal goes to the counter and asks for a form.	*Faiṣal yadhhab ilash shubbāk wa yaṭlub istimārah.*	فَيصَل يَذْهَبُ إِلَى الشُّبَّاك وَيَطْلُب اسْتِمَارَة.
Faisal: Please give me a form to open my account.	*Faiṣal: a'ṭinī istimārah lifatḥil ḥisāb min faḍlik.*	فَيصَل: أَعْطِنِي اسْتِمَارَة لِفَتْحِ الْحسَاب مِنْ فَضْلك.
Employee: Here it is, sir.	*al muwaẓẓaf: hādhihi hiyal istimārah, yā sayyidī.*	الْمُوَظَّف: هَذه هِي الاِسْتِمَارَة، يَا سَيِّدِي.

Faisal fills in the form and then gives it back to the bank employee.	*Faiṣal yamla' al istimārah thumma yurji'uhā ilal muwaẓẓaf.*	فَيصَل يَملَأ الاستمَارَة ثُمَّ يُرْجِعُهَا إِلَى الْمُوَظَّف.
Employee: You have not signed on the form. Please sign on it, sir.	*al muwaẓẓaf: mā waqqa'ta 'alal istimārah yā sayyidī. waqqi' 'alaihā dhālik min faḍlik.*	الْمُوَظَّف: مَا وَقَّعْتَ عَلَى الاسْتمَارَة يَا سَيِّدي. وقِّعْ عَلَيها مِنْ فَضْلك.
Faisal: Oh, sorry. I forgot to do it.	*Faiṣal: 'afwan, nasīt*	فَيْصَل: عَفْواً، نَسِيْت.
Employee: Thanks.	*al muwaẓẓaf: shukran*	الْمُوَظَّف: شُكْراً
Jamal: I have to withdraw some money from my account.	*Jamāl: urīd an asḥab ba'ḍan nuqūd min ḥisābī.*	جَمَال: أُرِيْدُ أَنْ أَسْحَب بَعْضَ النُّقُود مِن حِسَابي.
Employee: Have you signed on it?	*al muwaẓẓaf: hal waqqa'ta 'alal istimārah?*	الْمُوَظَّف: هَلْ وَقَّعْتَ عَلَى الاسْتمَارَة؟
Jamal: Yes, sir. Here is the cheque.	*Jamāl: na'am, yā sayyidī. hādhā huwash shīk.*	جَمَال: نَعَم، يَا سَيِّدي. هَذَا هُوَ الشّيْك.
The bank employee gives Jamal a token.	*yuqaddim muwaẓẓaful bank qasīmah ilā Jamāl.*	يُقدِّم مُوَظَّفُ الْبَنْك قَسِيمَة إِلَى جَمَال.
Employee: Take this token to counter no 12.	*al muwaẓẓaf: idhhab bihādhihil qasīmah ilash shubbāk raqm ithna 'ashara.*	الْمُوَظَّف: اذْهَبْ بِهَذه الْقَسِيْمَة إِلَى شُبَّاك رَقَم ١٢.
The employee at the counter 12: Token no. 556.	*muwaẓẓafush shubbāk raqm ithna 'ashara: qasīmah raqm sittuw wa khamsūn wa khams mi'ah.*	مُوَظَّفُ الشُّبَّاك رَقْمُ ١٢ : قَسِيمَة رَقْم ٥٥٦.
Jamal: Yes, sir.	*Jamāl: na'am yā sayyidī*	جَمَال: نَعَم، يَا سَيِّدي.
Employee: Take your amount.	*al muwaẓẓaf: hāk manshūdak.*	الْمُوَظَّف: هَاكَ مَنْشُودَك.
Jamal: Thank you.	*Jamāl: shukran*	جَمَال: شُكْراً

Employee: Not at all. We are at your service.	*al muwaẓẓaf: 'afwan. naḥnu fī khidmatikum.*	الْمُوَظَّف: عَفْواً. نَحْنُ فِي خِدْمَتِكُم.
Another person Fahad walks into the Bank and wants to encash his cheque.	*Fahad rajul ākhar yadkhul al bank li ṣarfi shīkihi.*	فَهْد رَجُل آخَر يَدْخُلُ الْبَنْك لِصَرْفِ شِيْكِه.
Fahad: I want to enchash this cheque, sir.	*Fahad: urīd ṣarfa hādhash shīk yā sayyidī.*	فَهْد: أُرِيْدُ صَرْفَ هَذَا الشِّيْك يَا سَيِّدي
Employee: What sort of cheque do you have?	*al muwaẓẓaf: ayyu shīk 'indak?*	الْمُوَظَّف: أيّ شِيْك عِنْدَك؟
Fahad: Crossed cheque.	*Fahad: shīk mu'anwan.*	فَهْد: شِيْك مُعَنْوَن .
Employee: Do you have your account in the bank?	*al muwaẓẓaf: hal laka ḥisāb fil bank?*	الْمُوَظَّف: هَلْ لَكَ حِسَاب فِي الْبَنْك؟
Fahad: Yes, I've a savings account in this bank.	*Fahad: na'am lī ḥisāb at taufīr fī hādhal bank.*	فَهْد: نَعَم، لِي حِسَابُ التَّوْفِيْر فِي هَذَا الْبَنْك.
Employee: Please submit the cheque in your account, the money will be transferred to your account.	*al muwaẓẓaf: rajā'an qaddimish shīk, taḥawwalun nuqūd ilā ḥisābik.*	الْمُوَظَّف: رَجَاءً قَدِّمِ الشِّيْك، تَحَوَّلُ النُّقُود إلَى حِسَابِك.
Fahad: Thank you.	*Fahad: shukran.*	فَهْد: شُكْراً
Employee: Here is the receipt. Anything else, sir?	*al muwaẓẓaf: hādhā huwal īṣāl. siyādatak shay'an ākhar?*	الْمُوَظَّف: هَذَا هُوَ الإِيْصَال. سِيَادَتُك شَيْئًا آخَر؟
Fahad: Yes, I also want to exchange some dollars. How can I get it done?	*Fahad: na'am, urīd an uḥawwil ba'ḍa dolārāt aiḍā. kaifa yumkinut taḥwīl ?*	فَهْد: نَعَم، أُرِيْد أنْ أُحَوِّل بَعْضَ دُولاَرَات أيْضاً. كَيْفَ يُمْكِنُ التَّحْوِيْل؟
Employee: For that you will have to go to the foreign exchange counter.	*al muwaẓẓaf: idhhab lidhālik ilā shubbāk al 'umlah al ajnabiyyah.*	الْمُوَظَّف: اذْهَبْ لِذَلك إلَى شُبَّاك الْعُمْلَة الأجْنَبِيَّة.

Fahad goes to that counter.	*Fahad yadhhab ilā dhālikash shubbāk.*	فَهْد يَذْهَبُ إِلَى ذَلكَ الشُّبَّاك.
Fahad: I want to exchange some currency.	*Fahad: urīd taḥwīla ba'ḍil 'umlah.*	فَهْد: أرِيْدُ تَحْوِيْلَ بَعْضِ الْعُمْلَة.
Employee: Which currency do you have?	*al muwaẓẓaf: ayyu'umlah 'indak?*	الْمُوَظَّف: أيُّ عُمْلَة عِنْدَك؟
Fahad: American dollar.	*Fahad: dolār amrīkiyy.*	فَهْد: دُولاَر أَمْرِيْكِي.
Employee: How many American dollars do you have?	*al-muwaẓẓaf: kam dolāran amrikiyyan 'indaka?*	الْمُوَظَّف: كَمْ دُولاَرًا أمْرِيْكِيًا عِنْدَك؟
Fahad: Five hundred	*Fahad: khamsu mi'ah*	فَهْد: خَمْسُ مِاْة.
Employee: please fill this form and submit it with your currnecy.	*almuwaẓẓaf: rajā'an imla' hādhihil istimārah wa qaddimhā ma'al 'umlah.*	الموظّف: رَجَاءً امْلأْ هَذه الاسْتِمَارَة وَقَدِّمْهَا مَعَ الْعُمْلَة.
Fahad fills the form and submits along with the currnecy to the bank employee at the counter.	*Fahad yamla'ul istimārah wa yuqaddimuhā ma'al 'umlah ilā muwaẓẓafil bank.*	فَهْد يَمْلأُ الاسْتمَارَة وَيُقَدِّمُهَا مَعَ الْعُمْلَة إِلَى مُوَظَّفِ الْبَنْك.
Fahad: Please sir, here is the form and 500 US dollars.	*Fahad: sayyidī hādhihi hiyal istimārah wa khams mi'ah dolar amrīkiyy.*	فَهْد: سَيِّدي، هَذه هِيَ الْاسْتمَارَة وَخَمْس مِأَة دُولاَر أمْرِيْكي.
Employee: Please collect your money. Here it is.	*al muwaẓẓaf: hādhihi hiya nūqūduk. khudhhā min faḍlik.*	الْمُوَظَّف: هَذه هِيَ نُقُودُك خُذْهَا مِنْ فَضْلك.
Fahad: Thanks.	*Fahad: shukran.*	فَهْد: شُكْراً.
Employee: you are welcome sir.	*al muwaẓẓaf: marḥabā yā sayyidi.*	الْمُوَظَّف: مَرْحَبًا يَا سَيِّدِي.

At the Post office

(*fī maktabil barīd*) فِي مَكْتَبِ الْبَرِيْد

Faisal: Where is the Post office, Fahad? Will you please guide me the way to the post office.	*Faiṣal: aina maktabul barīd yā Fahad ? hal tadullunī 'alaṭ ṭarīq al muwaddī ilā maktabil burīd min faḍlik?*	فَيصَل: أَيْنَ مَكْتَبُ الْبَرِيْد يَا فَهْد؟ هَلْ تَدُلُّنِي عَلَى الطَّرِيْقِ الْمُؤَدِّي إِلَى مَكْتَبِ الْبَرِيْد مِنْ فَضْلِك؟
Fahad: Yes, But why do you want to go there?	*Fahad: na'am, walākin lima turīd an tadhhab hunāk?*	فَهْد: نَعَم، وَلَكِنْ لِمَ تُرِيْد أَنْ تَذْهَب هُنَاك؟
Faisal: I want to buy some postal envelopes.	*Faiṣal: urīd an ashtariya ba'ḍaẓ ẓurūf al barīdiyyah.*	فَيصَل: أُرِيْد أَنْ اشترى بَعْضَ الظُّرُوف الْبَرِيْدِيَّة.
I have not sent any letter to my father for a long time.	*mā arsaltu ayya risālah ilā abī mundhu zamān.*	مَا أَرْسَلْتُ أَيَّ رِسَالَة إِلَى أَبِي مُنْذُ زَمَان.
He must be very anxious about me. I must inform him about my well being.	*la'allahu qaliq jiddā li ajlī. urīd an ukhbirahu bi'āfiyatī.*	لَعَلَّه قَلِق جِدًّا لِأَجْلِي. أُرِيْد أَن أُخْبِرَه بِعَافِيَتِي.
Is this Post office far away from here?	*hal hādhal maktab ba'īd min hunā?*	هَلْ هَذَا الْمَكْتَب بَعِيْد مِنْ هُنَا؟

Fahad: No, friend, it is very near. It is just beside the central bank.	*Fahad: lā, yā ṣadīqī, bal huwa qarīb jiddā. huwa bijiwāril bankil markaziyy.*	فَهْد: لاَ، يَا صَدِيْقِي، بَلْ هُوَ قَرِيْب جداً. هُوَ بِجِوَارِ الْبَنْك الْمَرْكَزِيّ.
It is only a ten minutes' walk from here.	*hādhā ya'khudh 'ashra daqā'iq faqaṭ mashyan 'alal aqdām.*	هَذَا يَأْخُذُ عَشْرَ دَقَائِق فَقَط مَشْيًا عَلَى الأَقْدَام.
Faisal: Is this a G.P.O.?	*Faiṣal: hal hādhal maktab maktab 'ām.*	فَيصَل: هَلْ هَذَا الْمَكْتَب مَكْتَب عَامّ؟
Fahad: Yes, brother. This is a General Post Office.	*Fahad: na'am yā ṣadīqī hādhal maktab maktab 'āmm.*	فَهْد: نَعَم، يَا صدِيْقِي هَذَا الْمَكْتَب مَكْتَب عَامّ.
Faisal: It means that all facilities are available in that post office.	*Faiṣal: ma'nāhu annahu yūjad fihi kullut tashīlāt.*	فَيصَل: مَعْنَاه أنّه يُوجَد فِيْه كُــلُّ التَّسْهِيْلاَت.
Fahad: Yes, you can send letters by ordinary mail or registered mail or speed post.	*Fahad: na'am yumkin lak an tursilal khiṭābāt bil barīd al 'ādī au bil barīd al musajjal au bil barīd assarī'.*	فَهْد: نَعَم، يُمْكِن لَكَ أَن تُرْسِلَ الْخطَابَات بِالْبَرِيْد الْعَادِي أَوْ بِالْبَرِيْد الْمُسَجَّل أَوْ بِالْبَرِيْد السَّرِيْع.
There are other facilities like parcels and telegraphs which are sent and delivered to all corners of the world.	*wa ghaira dhālik minat tashīlāt al ukhrā kaṭṭurūd wal barqiyyāt allatī tursal wa tūṣal ilā anḥā'il 'ālam.*	وَغَيْرَ ذَلك مِنَ التَّسْهِيْلاَت الأخرَى كَالطُّرُود وَالْبَرْقِيَّات الَّتِي تُرْسَل وَتُوصَل إِلَى أَنْحَاء الْعَالَم.
There are many counters in that post office and every counter offers a special service.	*fi dhālikal maktab shabābīk kathīrah, wa kullu shubbāk yuqaddimu khidmah mukhaṣṣaṣah.*	فِي ذَلك الْمَكْتَب شَبَابِيْك كَثِيْرَة وَكُلُّ شُبَّاك يُقَدِّمُ خِدْمَة مُخَصَّصَة.
There is a counter for selling envelopes, inland letters, cards and stamps, a counter for sending letters and parcels; and a counter for postal orders.	*hunāk shubbāk libai'iẓ ẓurūf wal makātīb addākhiliyyah wal biṭāqāt wa ṭawābi'il barīd. wa shubbāk li irsālil khiṭābāt waṭṭurūd, wa shubbāk lil ḥawālāt al māliyah.*	هُنَاكَ شُبَّاك لِبَيْعِ الظُّرُوف وَالْمَكَاتِيْب الدَّاخلِيَّة وَالْبطَاقَات وَطَوَابِع الْبَرِيْد، وَشُبَّاك لِإِرْسَال الْخطَابَات وَالطُّرُوْد، وَشُبَّاك لِلْحَوَالاَت الْمَالِيَّة.

Fahad: I'm also going to the Post Office. Would you like to come with me?	*Fahad: anā aiḍan adhhab ilā maktabil barīd. hal tawadd an tuṣāḥibanī?*	فَهْد: أنَا أيْضًا أذْهَبُ إِلَى مَكْتَبِ الْبَرِيْدِ. هَلْ تَوَدّ أَنْ تُصَاحِبَنِي؟
Faisal: Oh, sure.	*Faiṣal: ay na'am.*	فَيْصَل: أي، نَعَم.
They enter the Post Office building.	*humā yadkhulāni mabnā maktabil barīd.*	هُمَا يَدْخُلاَنِ مَبْنَى مَكْتَبِ الْبَرِيْد.
Post Office employee: what can I do for you, sir?	*muwaẓẓafu maktabil barīd: ayya khidmah yā sayyidī?*	مُوَظَّفُ مَكْتَبِ الْبَرِيْد: أيّ خِدْمَة يَا سَيِّدِي؟
Faisal: I would like to have five envelopes, three inland letters and ten cards.	*Faiṣal: urīdu an ākhudh khamsata ẓurūf wa thalāthata makātīb dākhiliyyah wa 'ashara biṭāqāt.*	فَيصَل: أُرِيْد أَنْ آخُذ خَمْسَةَ ظُرُوف وَثَلاثَةَ مَكَاتِيْب دَاخِلِيَّة وَعَشْرَ بِطَاقَات.
Employee: You have to pay thirty pounds.	*al muwaẓẓaf: idfa' thalāthīna junaihā yā sayyidī.*	الْمُوَظَّف: ادْفَعْ ثَلاثِيْنَ جُنَيْهًا يَا سَيِّدِي.
Faisal: I would also like to have stamps worth ten pounds.	*Faiṣal: urīd an ākhudh ṭawābi' bi'asharah junaihāt aiḍan.*	فَيْصَل: أُرِيْد أَنْ آخُذ طَوَابِع بِعَشْرَة جُنَيْهَات أيْضاً.
Employee: What do you need this stamp for? Do you want to send a parcel.	*al muwaẓẓaf: li ayyi shay'? hal turīd an tursil ṭardan?*	الْمُوَظَّف: لأيِّ شَيْء؟ هَلْ تُرِيْد أَنْ تُرْسِل طَرْدًا؟
Faisal: No, but I want to send an Aerogram.	*Faiṣal: lā, bal urīd irsāla maktūb khārjiyy.*	فَيصَل: لاَ، بَلْ أُرِيْدُ إِرْسَال مَكْتُوب خَارِجِي.
Employee: By an ordinary mail or a registered mail?	*al muwaẓẓaf: bil barīd al 'āmm am bil barīd al musajjal?*	الْمُوَظَّف: بِالْبَرِيْد الْعَام أَمْ بِالْبَرِيْد الْمُسَجَّل؟
Faisal: By a registered mail. How much will I have to pay for this?	*Faiṣal: bil barīd al musajjal. kam yukallifunī hādhā?*	فَيصَل: بِالْبَرِيْد الْمُسَجَّل. كَمْ يُكَلِّفُنِي هَذَا؟
Employee: Twenty pounds, sir.	*al muwaẓẓaf: idfa' 'ishrīna junaihā yā sayyidī.*	الْمُوَظَّف: ادْفَع عِشْرِيْنَ جُنَيْهًا يَا سَيِّدِي.
Faisal: Here are twenty pounds.	*Faiṣal: hāk 'ishrīna junaihā.*	فَيْصَل: هَاكَ عِشْرِيْنَ جُنَيْهًا.

Employee: Please take this receipt.	*al muwaẓẓaf: khudhil īṣāl min faḍlik.*	الْمُوَظَّف: خُذْ الإيْصَال مِنْ فَضْلك.
Faisal: Thank you.	*Faiṣal: shukran.*	فَيصَل: شُكْراً.
Employee: Not at all.	*Al muwaẓẓaf: 'afwā.*	الْمُوَظَّف: عَفْواً.

Parcels Counter

(shubbākuṭṭurūd) شُبَّاكُ الطُّرُوْد

Employee: What do you want?	*al muwaẓẓaf: mādhā turīd?*	الْمُوَظَّف: مَاذَا تُرِيْد؟
Fahad: I want to send this parcel.	*Fahad: urīd irsāl hādhaṭ ṭard.*	فَهْد: أُرِيْد إرسَالَ هَذَا الطَّرْد.
Employee: By air mail or surface mail?	*al muwaẓẓaf: bil barīd al jawwī am bil barīd as saṭḥī?*	الْمُوَظَّف: بالْبَرِيْد الْجَوِّي أَمْ بالْبَرِيْد السَّطْحِي؟
Fahad: By surface mail.	*Fahad: bil barīd assaṭḥī.*	فَهْد: بِالْبَرِيْد السَّطْحِي.
Employee: What is the weight of your parcel?	*al muwaẓẓaf: kam waznu ṭardik?*	الْمُوَظَّف: كَمْ وَزْنُ طَرْدك؟
Fahad: One and a half kg. How much do I have to pay?	*Fahad: kīlo gharām wa niṣf. kam uwaddī?*	فَهْد: كِيْلو غِرَام وَنِصْف. كَمْ أُوَدِّي؟
Employee: Two pounds only.	*al- muwaẓẓaf: junaihain faqaṭ.*	الْمُوَظَّف: جُنَيْهَيْن فَقَط.
Fahad: Thank you.	*Fahad: shukran.*	فَهْد: شُكْراً.

Postal order

(ḥawālah māliyah) حَوَالَة مَالِيَّة

Jamal: Good evening.	*Jamāl: masā'al khair.*	جَمَال: مَسَاءَ الْخَيْر.
Employee: Good evening. What can I do for you?	*al muwaẓẓaf: masā'an nūr. ayya khidmah?*	الْمُوَظَّف: مَسَاءَ النُّوْر. أيّ خِدْمَة؟
Jamal: I want to send a postal order.	*Jamāl: urīd irsāla ḥawālah māliyah.*	جَمَال: أُرِيْد إرْسَال حَوَالَة مَالِيَّة.

Employee: Where do you want to send it?	*al muwazzaf: ilā aina turīd an tursilahā ?*	الْمُوَظَّف: إِلَى أَيْنَ تُرِيْد أَنْ تُرْسِلَهَا؟
Jamal: To Cairo.	*Jamāl: ilal qāhirah.*	جَمَال: إِلَى الْقَاهِرَة.
Employee: What is the amount you want to send?	*al muwazzaf: kamil mablagh alladhī turīd irsālahu?*	الْمُوَظَّف: كَمِ الْمَبْلَغ الَّذِي تُرِيْدُ إِرْسَالَه؟
Jamal: One thousand pounds.	*Jamāl: alfu junaih.*	جَمَال: أَلْف جُنَيْه.
How much is the postal charge for sending this money?	*mā huwa ajrul barīd li irsāli hādhal mablagh?*	مَا هُوَ أَجْرُ الْبَرِيْد لإِرْسَال هَذَا الْمَبْلَغ؟
Employee: Twenty five pounds by ordinary mail. Please fill this form, sir.	*al muwazzaf : khamsatuw wa 'ishrūna junaihā bil barīd al 'āmm. rajā'an imla' hādhihil istimārah, sayyidī.*	الْمُوَظَّف: خَمْسَةٌ وَّعِشْرُونَ جُنَيْهًا بِالْبَرِيْد الْعَام. رَجَاءً امْلأْ هَذِهِ الاسْتِمَارَة، سَيِّدِي.
Jamal: Alright.	*Jamāl: ḥasanan.*	جَمَال: حَسَنًا.
Employee: Sender's signature is not there on it. Please sign on it, sir.	*al muwazzaf: laisa 'alaihi tauqī'ul mursil waqqi' 'alā dhālik min faḍlik yā sayyidī.*	الْمُوَظَّف: لَيْسَ عَلَيْه تَوقِيْعُ الْمُرْسِل، وَقِّعْ عَلَى ذَلِكَ مِنْ فَضْلِك يَا سَيِّدِي.
Jamal: Oh, sorry.	*Jamāl: ay āsif.*	جَمَال: أَي آسِف.
And here is the money with the postal charges.	*hādhā huwal mablagh wa hādhihi hiyal ujrah al barīdiyyah.*	هَذَا هُوَ الْمَبْلَغ وَهَذِه هِيَ الأُجْرَة الْبَرِيْدِيَّة.
Employee: Please have your receipt.	*al muwazzaf: khudhil īṣāl min faḍlik.*	الْمُوَظَّف: خُذ الإِيْصَال مِنْ فَضْلِك.
Jamal: Thank you.	*Jamāl: shukran.*	جَمَال: شُكْرًا.

In a Shopping Mall

(fī maḥallāt tijāriyyah) فِي مَحَلاَّت تِجَارِيَّة

Jamal and his wife are in a big shopping mall situated in the heart of the capital.	*Jamāl wa zawjatuhu fī sūq wāqi'ah fī qalbil 'āṣimah.*	جَمَال وَزَوْجَتُه فِيْ سُوقٍ وَاقِعَة فِي قَلْبِ الْعَاصِمَة.
There are many shops in this mall.	*hunāka maḥallāt kathīrah fī hādhihis sūq.*	هُنَاكَ مَحَلاَّت كَثِيْرَة فِي هَذِه السُّوْق.
Some shops are especially for woven and silk clothes, a few are for toys and home accessories, and there is a big grocer's shop.	*ba'ḍul maḥallāt khuṣūṣan lil mansūjāt wal ḥarīr wa ba'ḍuhā lilu'abil aṭfāl wa lil adawātil manziliyyah wa hunāka baqqālah kabīrah.*	بَعْضُ الْمَحَلاَّت خُصُوصاً لِلْمَنْسُوجَات وَالْحَرِيْر، وَبَعْضُهَا لِلُعَب الأَطْفَال وَللأدَوَات الْمَنْزِلِيَّة، وَهُنَاك بقَالَـة كَبِيْرَة.

In the Clothes Shop

(fī maḥallil malābis) فِي مَحَلِّ الْمَلاَبِس

Jamal and his wife enter the clothes shop. The owner of	*yadkhulu Jamāl wa zaujatuh fī maḥallil malābis*	يَدْخُلُ جَمَال وَزَوْجَتُه فِي مَحَلِّ الْمَلاَبِس فَيُرَحِّبُهُمَا

the shop warmly welcomes them and the following conversation goes between them:	*fayuraḥḥibuhumā ṣāḥibuh bi ṭalāqatil wajh, wa yajrī bainahumā al ḥadīth kal ātī.*	صَاحِبُه بِطَلاَقَة الْوَجْه وَيَجْرِى بَيْنَهُما الْحَدِيْث كَالآتِي:
Shop owner: Can I help you, sir?	*ṣāḥibul maḥall: ayy musā'adah yā sayyidī?*	صَاحِبُ الْمَحَلّ: أيّ مُسَاعَدَة يَا سَيِّدِي؟
Jamal: Can you show me some shirts and pants?	*Jamāl: hal tuqaddim ba'ḍal qumṣān wal banṭlūn?*	جَمَال: هَلْ تُقَدِّمُ بَعْضَ الْقُمْصَان وَالْبَنْطلُون؟
Jamal: Yes, please.	*Jamāl: na'am, min faḍlik.*	جَمَال: نَعَم، مِنْ فَضْلك.
Shop owner: What size fits you?	*ṣāḥibul maḥall: ayyu maqās yunāsibuka?*	صَاحِبُ الْمَحَلّ: أيُّ مَقَاس يُنَاسِبُك؟
Jamal: size 40 in shirt and 30 in pants.	*Jamāl: maqās raqm arba'ūn lil qamīṣ wa thalāthūn lil banṭlūn.*	جَمَال: مَقَاس رَقْم ٤٠ لِلْقَمِيْصِ وَ ٣٠ لِلْبَنْطلُون
Shop owner: Please come inside, sir. They are all size 40. The quality of these shirts is good. They are pure cotton shirts.	*ṣāḥibul maḥall: tafaḍḍal yā sayyidī hādhihi kulluhā maqās raqm arba'ūn, nau'u hādhihil qumṣān jayyid, wa hādhihi kulluhā quṭn aṣlī.*	صَاحِبُ الْمَحَلّ: تَفَضَّلْ يَا سَيِّدِي. هَذه كُلُّهَا مَقَاس رَقْم ٤٠، نَوْعُ هَذه الْقُمْصَان جَيِّد، وَهَذه كُلُّهَا قُطْن أَصْلِي
Jamal: How much are these?	*Jamāl: kam thamanuhā?*	جَمَال: كَمْ ثَمَنُهَا؟
Shop owner: These are for fifty pounds.	*ṣāḥibul maḥall: thamanuhā khamsūna junaihā.*	صَاحِبُ الْمَحَلّ: ثَمَنُهَا خَمْسُون جُنَيْهًا.
Jamal: Give me two shirts, please.	*Jamāl: a'ṭinī qamīṣain min faḍlik*	جَمَال: أَعْطِنِى قَمِيْصَيْن مِن فَضْلك.
Do you have towels also?	*hal 'indak manāshif aiḍan?*	هَلْ عِنْدَك مَنَاشِف أيْضاً؟
Shop owner: Yes, we do. What colour would you like?	*ṣāḥibul maḥall: na'am, wa ayya laun turīd?*	صَاحِبُ الْمَحَلّ: نَعَم، وَأيّ لَون تُرِيْد؟
Jamal: Yellow.	*Jamāl: laun aṣfar.*	جَمَال: لَون أَصْفَر.

Shop owner: Here is the yellow towel for you, sir. This is for twenty pounds.	*ṣāḥibul maḥall: hāk minshafah ṣafrā' yā sayyidī. thamanuhā 'ishrūna junaihā.*	صَاحِبُ الْمَحَلّ: هَاكَ مِنْشَفَة صَفْرَاء يَا سَيِّدِي ثَمَنُهَا عِشْرُون جُنَيْهاً.
Jamal: Do you have shoes?	*Jamāl: hal 'indakum aḥdhiyah?*	جَمَال: هَلْ عِنْدَكُم أحْذِيَة؟
Shop owner: Yes, sir. We have some very good quality shoes.	*ṣāḥibul maḥall: na'am, yā sayyidī. 'indanā aḥdhiyah min nau'iyah mumtāzah.*	صَاحِبُ الْمَحَلّ: نَعَم، يَا سَيِّدِي. عِنْدَنَا أَحْذِيَة مِنْ نَوْعِيَة مُمْتَازَة.
Jamal: Show me that black one.	*Jamāl: arinī tilkas saudā'.*	جَمَال: أَرِنِي تِلْكَ السَّوْدَاء.
Shop owner: Anything for you, madam?	*ṣāḥibul maḥall: wa ayyu shay' laki yā sayyidatī?*	صَاحِبُ الْمَحَلّ: وَأَيُّ شَيْء لَكِ يَا سَيِّدَتِي؟
Maryam: yes, I want to purchase four metre woven clothes and four metre silk clothes.	*Maryam: na'am, urīd an ashtariya arba'ata amtār nasījan wa arba'ata amtār ḥarīran.*	مَرِيَم: نَعَم، أرِيْدُ أَنْ أَشْتَرِى أربَعَةَ أمْتَار نَسِيْجاً وَأَرْبَعَةَ أَمْتَار حَرِيْراً.
Shop owner: Here are your clothes, madam.	*ṣāḥibul maḥall: khudh malābisak sayyidatī.*	صَاحِبُ الْمَحَلّ: خُذْ مَلاَبِسَك سَيِّدَتِي.
Maryam: How much are these?	*Maryam: kam thamanuhā?*	مَرِيَم: كَم ثَمَنُهَا؟
Shop owner: Twenty pounds.	*ṣāḥibul maḥall: 'ishrūna junaihan.*	صَـاحِبُ الْمَحَلّ: عِشْرُون جُنَيْهاً.
Maryam: Here are twenty pounds. Thank you.	*Maryam: hādhihi hiya 'ishrūn junaihan, shukran.*	مَرْيَم: هَذه هِيَ عِشْرُون جُنَيْهًا، شُكْراً
Shop owner: you are welcome.	*ṣāḥibul maḥall: marḥabā.*	صَاحِبُ الْمَحَلّ: مَرحَبًا

In a Grocery

(fī biqālah) فِي بِقَالَة

Grocer: What do you want, madam?	*al baqqāl: mādhā turīdīna yā sayyidatī?*	الْبَقَّال: مَاذَا تُرِيْدِيْن يَا سَيِّدَتِي؟
Maryam: A toothbrush and a toothpaste.	*Maryam: furshātal asnān wa ma'jūnal asnān.*	مَرِيَم: فُرشَاةَ الأَسْنَان وَمَعْجُونَ الأَسْنَان.

Grocer: All right, madam. Anything else?	*al baqqāl: ḥasanan, sayyidati. wa ayya shay' ākhar?*	البَقّال: حَسَنًا، سَيِّدَتِي. وَأيّ شَيءٍ آخَر؟
Maryam: yes, I've a complete list of things.	*Maryam: na'am, 'indi qā'imatul ashyā' kāmilatan.*	مَريَم: نَعَم، عِندي قَائمَة الأشْيَاء كَامِلةً.
Grocer: Can I take this list?	*al baqqāl: hal ākhudh al qā'imah?*	البَقّال: هَلْ آخُذ الْقَائمَة؟
Maryam: Oh, yes, here it is.	*Maryam: ay na'am, hādhihi hiya.*	مَريَم: أي نَعَم، هَذه هِيَ.
Grocer reads from the list and says to his assistant:	*al baqqāl yaqra' al qā'imah wa ya'mur musā'idahu.*	الْبَقّال يَقْرأ الْقَائمَة وَيَأمُر مُسَاعدَه:
Bring butter 200g. jam 1/2 k.g. soap 2 pc. shaving cream 1pc.	*hāti zubdah mi'atai ghirām murabbā niṣf kiloghirām ṣābūn ḥabbatain ma'jūnul ḥilāqah ḥabbah.*	هَات زُبْدَة ٢٠٠ غِرَام، مُربَّى نِصْف كِيْلُو غرَام، صَابُون حَبَّتَيْن، مَعْجُون الْحلاقَة حَبَّة .
Grocer: Please pay forty pounds at the counter in the corner. You can collect your things from the counter next to it.	*al baqqāl: idfa'ī arba'īna junaihan 'alash shubbāk fin nāḥiyah wa khudhil ashyā' minash shubbāk al mubāshir.*	البَقّال: ادْفَعِي أرْبَعِيْن جُنَيْهاً عَلَى الشُّبَّاك فِي النَّاحيَة وَخُذِي الأشْيَاء مِنَ الشُّبَّاك الْمُبَاشِر.
Maryam: Thank you.	*Maryam: shukran*	مَريَم: شُكْراً
Maryam: We must buy a balloon for Saeed	*Maryam: yajib an nashtariya bālūnan li Sa'īd.*	مَريَم: يَجِب أنْ نَشْتَرِى بِالُوناً لِسَعِيْد.
Jamal: yes, sure my dear.	*Jamāl: ay na'am, yā ḥabībatī.*	جَمَال: أيْ نَعَم، يَا حَبِيْبَتِي.
But we must also have something before we head for the toy shop. I am feeling so hungry.	*walākin lina'khudh shay'an qabla an natawajjah ilā maḥallil lu'ab, innanī ash'ur bil jū' ash shadīd.*	وَلَكنْ لِنَأخُذْ شَيْئًا قَبْلَ أنْ نَتَوجَّه إلَى مَحَلّ اللُّعَب، إنَّنِي أشْعُر بِالْجُوع الشَّدِيْد.
Maryam: Oh, yes dear. I am also feeling hungry.	*Maryam: ay na'am ya ḥabīb anā aiḍan jau'ā.*	مَريَم: أيْ نَعَم، يَا حَبِيْبِي أنَا أيْضاً جَوعَى.

Jamal: Then let us to go to that restaurant.	*Jamāl: falnadhhab ilā dhālikal maqṣaf.*	جَمَال: فَلْنَذْهَب إِلَى ذَلِكَ الْمَقْصَف.
Their younger son Saeed was waiting for his parents at home. When parents gave him balloon and chocolates his happiness knew no bounds.	*ibnuhumaṣ ṣaghīr kāna yantaẓiru wālidaihi fil bait 'indama a'ṭāhu wālidāhu al bālūna wash shokolāt fariḥa farḥan shadīdā.*	ابْنُهُمَا الصَّغِيْر كَانَ يَنْتَظِرُ وَالِدَيْه فِي الْبَيْت، عِنْدَمَا أَعْطَاه وَالِدَاه الْبَالُون وَالشُّوكُولات فَرِحَ فَرْحًا شَدِيْداً.

The Hospital

(*almustashfā*) الْمُسْتَشْفَى

Nasir: What happened, brother?	*Naṣir: mādhā ḥadatha yā akhī?*	نَاصِر: مَاذَا حَدَثَ يَا أخِي؟
Jamal: My brother has met with an accident.	*Jamāl: qad uṣība akhī bi ḥādithah.*	جَمَال: قَدْ أُصِيبَ أخِي بِحَادِثَة.
Nasir: How did it happen?	*Nāṣir: kaifa kāna dhālik?*	نَاصِر: كَيْفَ كَانَ ذَلِك؟
Jamal: He was going with his family when a bus hit his car.	*Jamāl: ḥīnamā kāna yadhhab ma'a 'ā'ilatihi ṣadama ūtūbuṣ sayyāratahu.*	جَمَال: حِيْنَمَا كَانَ يَذْهَب مَعَ عَائِلَتِه صَدَمَ أُوتُوبُص سَيَّارَته.
Nasir: Has he suffered any injuries?	*Nāsir: awa uṣība bijurūḥ*	نَاصِر: أَوَ أُصِيبَ بِجُرُوح؟
Jamal: Yes, there may be some fractures.	*Jamāl: na'am, wa yumkin an takūna hunāk kusūr.*	جَمَال: نَعَم، وَيُمْكِن أنْ تَكُونَ هُنَاكَ كُسُور.
Nasir: And what about his family?	*Nāṣir: wa kaifa ḥālu usratih?*	نَاصِر: وَكَيْفَ حَالُ أُسْرَتِه؟

Jamal: They are safe by the grace of Allah.	*Jamāl: hum sālimūn bi faḍlillāh.*	جَمَال: هُمْ سَالِمُون بِفَضْلِ الله.
Nasir: Which hospital are you taking him to?	*Nāṣir: ilā ayy mustashfā tadhhab bih?*	نَاصر: إلَى أيّ مُسْتَشْفَى تَذْهَب بِه؟
Jamal: To a hospital located at the William Road.	*Jamāl: ilal mustashfā al wāqi' bi shāri' wiliam.*	جَمَال: إلَى الْمُسْتَشْفَى الْوَاقِع بشَارِع وِلْيَم.
Nasir: Is that a big hospital?	*Nāṣir: hal dhālika mustashfā kabīr?*	نَاصر: هَل ذَلكَ مُسْتَشْفَى كَبِيْر؟
Jamal: Yes it is a big and well-known hospital. It has all facilities.	*Jamāl: na'am huwa mustashfā kabīr wa shahīr wa yatawaffar fihi jamī'ut tashīlāt.*	جَمَال: نَعَم هُوَ مُسْتَشْفَى كَبِيْر وَشَهِيْر، وَ يَتَوفَّر فِيْه جَمِيْعُ التَّسْهِيلاَت.
Nasir: Does it have an Orthopedics Department?	*Nāṣir: hal yūjad fihi qismut tajbīr?*	نَاصر: هَلْ يُوجَد فِيْه قِسْمُ التَّجْبِيْر؟
Jamal: Yes, it does. Besides, it has many other departments, like, Dental, Eyes, Skin, Heart, and Gyno.	*Jamāl: na'am, yūjad fihi tajbīrul 'iẓām. wa bil iḍāfah ilā dhālik tūjad hunāk aqsām kathīrah kaqism lil asnān wa qism lil 'uyūn wa qism lil julūd wa qism lil qalb wa qism lil amrāḍin nisā'iyyah.*	جَمَال: نَعَم، يُوجَد فِيْه تَجْبِيْرُ الْعظَام. وَبالإضَافَة إلَى ذَلك تُوجَد هُنَاك أقْسَام كَثِيْرَة كَقِسْم للأَسْنَان وَقِسْم للعُيُون وَقِسْم لَلْجُلُود وَقِسْم لِلْقَلْبِ وَقِسْم لِلأمْرَاضِ النِّسَائِيَّة.
All the departments are fully equipped with most modern facilities and each department has many specialists.	*kullu qism muzawwad bi aḥdathit tashīlāt wa fi kulli qism hunāk kathīrum minal ikhṣā'iyyīn.*	كُلُّ قِسْم مُزَوَّد بأحْدَث التَّسْهِيْلاَت وَفِي كُلِّ قِسْم هُنَاك كَثِيْر مِنَ الإخْصَائِيِّيْن.
Nasir: Is there an emergency ward there?	*Nāṣir: hal yūjad hunāk qism liṭṭawārī?*	نَاصر: هَلْ يُوجَد هُنَاك قِسْم للطَّوَارِي؟
Jamal: Yes, there is an emergency ward which is open 24 hours.	*Jamāl: na'am hunāk qism liṭṭawārī maftūḥ arba'an wa 'ishrīna sā'ah*	جَمَال: نَعَم هُنَاكَ قِسْم لِلطَّوَارِي مَفْتُوح أرْبَعاً وَّ عِشْرِيْنَ سَاعَة.

It also provides ambulance service in emergency.	*wa huwa yuqaddim khidmatal is'āf fiṭṭawārī.*	وَهُوَ يُقَدِّم خِدْمَةَ الإِسْعَاف فِي الطَّوَارِي.
Nasir: Can I come along with you?	*Nāṣir: hal amshī ma'ak?*	نَاصِر: هَل أَمْشِي مَعَك؟
Jamal: Yes, you can. We must take him to the hospital as fast as possible.	*Jamāl: na'am, hayyā nadhhab bih ilal mustashfā fi asra'i waqt mumkin.*	جَمَال: نَعَم، هَيَّا نَذْهَب بِه إِلَى الْمُسْتَشْفَى فِي أَسْرَع وَقْت مُمْكِن.
Jamal takes his injured brother to the hospital. Nasir also accompanies him.	*yadhhab Jamāl bi akhīhil jarīḥ ilal mustashfā wa yuṣāḥibuh Nāṣir aiḍan.*	يَذْهَب جَمَال بِأَخِيْه الْجَرِيْح إِلَى الْمُسْتَشْفَى وَيُصَاحِبُه نَاصِر أَيْضاً.
Jamal goes to the reception: Can you please send a stretcher outside.	*Jamāl yaḍhab ilā muwaẓẓafil isti'lāmāt: hal tursil naqqālah ilal khārij min faḍlik?*	جَمَال يَذْهَب إِلَي مُوَظَّف الاسْتِعْلاَمَات: هَلْ تُرسِل نَقَّالَة إِلَى الْخَارِج مِنْ فَضْلك؟
Receptionist: Oh yes, sure.	*al muwaẓẓaf: ay na'am wa bitta'kīd.*	الْمُوَظَّف: أي نَعَم، وَ بالتَّأكِيْد.
Jamal: which way is the orthopaedics?	*Jamāl: aina tajbīrul 'iẓām?*	جَمَال، أَيْنَ تَجْبِيْرُ الْعِظَام؟
Receptionist: Go first left.	*al muwaẓẓaf: awwalan idhhab shimālak.*	الْمُوَظَّف: أَوَّلاً اذْهَب شِمَالَك.
Jamal: Is the doctor in?	*Jamāl: haliṭṭabīb maujūd fiddākhil?*	جَمَال: هَلِ الطَّبِيْب مَوْجُود فِي الدَّاخِل؟
Nurse: Yes, he is examining a patient. Please wait until he has finished.	*al mumarriḍah: na'am huwa yakshif 'alā marīḍin, intaẓir ḥattā yafarugh.*	الْمُمَرِّضَة: نَعَم، هُوَ يَكْشِف عَلَى مَرِيْض، انْتَظِر حَتَّى يَفْرُغ.
Doctor: What is wrong with you?	*aṭṭabīb: mādhā aṣābak yā akhī?*	الطَّبِيْب: مَاذَا أَصَابَك يَا أَخِي؟
Patient: I suffered some injuries in my right leg in a road accident a few minutes back.	*almarīḍ: uṣibtu bijurūḥ fi rijlil yumnā fi ḥādithis sayyārah qabla daqā'iq.*	الْمَرِيْض: أُصِبْتُ بِجُرُوح فِي رِجْلِي الْيُمْنَى فِي حَادِث السَّيَّارَة قَبْلَ دَقَائِق.

Doctor: Do not get upset. Go and get your leg x-rayed and then come back again with the report.	*aṭṭabīb: lā taqlaq, idhhab wa akmil ijrā'ātil ashi''ah wa rāji' marrah ukhrā ma'attaqrīr.*	الطَّبِيْب: لاَ تَقْلَق، اذْهَب وَأَكْمِل إجْرَاءَات الأَشعَّة وَرَاجِع مَرَّة أخرَى مَعَ التَّقرِيْر.
Jamal takes his brother on stretcher to x-ray department. On the way, they pass through a big hall.	*Jamāl yanqul akhāhu ilā qismil ashi''ah 'alan naqqālah wa fiṭṭarīq hum yamurrūn bi qā'ah kabīrah.*	جَمَال يَنْقُل أخَاه إلَى قِسْم الأَشعَّة عَلَى النَّقَّالَة وَفِي الطَّرِيْق هُمْ يَمُرُّوْنَ بِقَاعَة كَبِيْرَة.
Nasir: What is this big hall for, brother?	*Nāṣir: wa mā hādhihiṣ ṣālah al kabīrah yā akh?*	نَاصِر: وَمَا هَذه الصَّالَة الْكَبِيْرَة يَا أَخ؟
Jamal: It is a pathology department of the hospital, the blood, urine and stool are tested here.	*Jamāl: hādhā qismul bātholojiyā, hunā yajrī faḥṣud dam wal baul wal barāz.*	جَمَال: هَذَا قِسْم الْبَاثُولُوجيا، هُنَا يجْرِى فَحْص الدَّم وَالْبَوْل وَالْبَرَاز.
Nasir: Is there a pharmacy also in this hospital?	*hal tūjad ṣaydaliyyah aiḍan fī hādhal mustashfā?*	نَاصِر: هَل تُوجَدُ صَيْدَلِيَّة أيْضاً فِي هَذَا الْمُسْتَشْفَى؟
Jamal: Yes, there is a big pharmacy also here.	*Jamāl: na'am hunā ṣaydaliyyah kabīrah aiḍan.*	جَمَال: نَعَم، هُنَا صَيْدَلِيَّة كَبِيْرَة أيْضاً.
Nasir: Thank you, brother, for such useful information.	*Nāṣir: shukran, yā akh 'alā hādhihil ma'lūmāt al mufīdah.*	نَاصِر: شُكْراً، يَا أخ عَلَى هَذه الْمَعْلُومَات الْمُفِيْدَة.

A Holiday
(yaumul ʻuṭlah) يَوْمُ العُطْلَة

Nasir: Where are you going to spend your holiday?	*Nāṣir: ain tadhhab liqaḍā'i yaumi ʻuṭlatik?*	ناصر: أيْنَ تَذْهَب لِقضَاءِ يَوْمِ عُطْلَتك؟
Jamal: We are going to visit a park.	*Jamāl: nadhhab liziyārati ḥadīqah.*	جَمَال: نَذْهَب لِزِيَارَة حَدِيْقَة.
Nasir: Which park?	*Nāṣir: ilā ayyi ḥadīqah?*	ناصر: إلَى أيِّ حَدِيْقَة؟
Jamal: The National Park which is situated on the riverside. It is a big and beautiful park.	*Jamāl: ilal ḥadīqah al qaumiyyah alwāqiʻah ʻalā ḍiffatin nahr, innahā ḥadīqah kabīrah wa jamīlah.*	جَمَال: إلَى الْحَدِيْقَة الْقَوْمِيَّة الْوَاقِعَة عَلَى ضِفَّة النَّهْر، إنَّهَا حَدِيْقَة كَبِيْرَة وَجَمِيْلَة.
Nasir: Are you going there with your family?	*Nāṣir: hal tadhhab hunāk maʻa usratik?*	ناصر: هَلْ تَذْهَب هُنَاكَ مَعَ أُسْرَتك؟
Jamal: Yes.	*Jamāl: nāʻam*	جَمَال: نَعَم.
Naṣir: Do you go to the park every Sunday?	*Nāṣir: hal tadhhab ilal ḥadīqah kulla yumil aḥad?*	ناصر: هَلْ تَذْهَب إلَى الْحَدِيْقَة كُلَّ يَوْم الأحَد؟
Jamal: No, not every Sunday.	*Jamāl: lā' lā nadhhab kulla yaumil aḥad.*	جَمَال: لاَ، لاَ نَذْهَب كُلَّ يَومِ الأحَد.

Sometimes we go out on the beach and sometimes we go out to visit some of the friends or relatives. Sometimes we stay in our house and invite our friends and relatives.	*ba'ḍal aḥyān nakhruj ilā shāṭi'il baḥr wa ba'ḍal aḥyān nakhruj liziyārati ba'ḍil aṣdiqā' awil aqribā' wa aḥyānan nabqā fil bait wa nad'ū aṣdiqā'anā wa aqāribanā.*	بَعْضَ الأَحْيَان نَخْرُج إِلَى شَاطِئ الْبَحْر وَبَعْض الأَحْيَان نَخْرُج لِزِيَارَة بَعْضِ الأَصْدِقَاء أَو الأَقْرِبَاء وَأَحْيَاناً نَبْقَى فِي الْبَيْت وَنَدْعُو أَصْدِقَاءَنَا وَأَقَارِبَنَا.
Jamal gets the tickets and enters the park with his family. The park is crowded with men, women and children. They are all enjoying in the park.	*Jamāl yashtarit tadhākir wa yadkhul al ḥadīqah ma'a usratih, al ḥadīqah mal'ānah bir rijāl wan nisā' wal aṭfāl wa kulluhum yatamatta'ūn fil ḥadīqah.*	جَمَال يَشْتَرِى التَّذَاكِر وَيَدْخُل الْحَدِيْقَة مَعَ أُسْرَته، الْحَدِيْقَة مَلآنَة بِالرِّجَال وَالنِّسَاء وَالأَطْفَال وَكُلُّهُم يَتَمَتَّعُون فِي الْحَدِيْقَة.
The weather inside the park is pleasant and the wind is fine. The park has beautiful fountains which add to its beauty.	*al jaww bidākhilihā laṭīf wal hawā' fīhā naqiy, wa hunāk nawāfir jamīlah wa hiya tazīd fī jamālihā.*	اَلْجَوّ بِدَاخِلِهَا لَطِيْف وَالْهَوَاء فِيْهَا نَقِيّ، وَهُنَاك نَوَافِيْر جَمِيْلَة وَهِيَ تَزِيْدُ فِي جَمَالِهَا.
The children are playing around the fountains and they all look very happy. Their parents are sitting on the green lawns of the park and chatting. Some children are playing with the balloons.	*al aṭfāl yal'abūna ḥaulan nawāfir wa hum fariḥūn, ābā'uhum wa ummahātuhum jālisūna fī makhḍaratil ḥadīqah wa yataḥādathūn, ba'ḍul aṭfāl yal'abūn bil bālūnāt.*	الأَطْفَال يَلْعَبُون حَوْلَ النَّوَافِيْر وَهُم فَرِحُون، آبَاءُهُم وَأُمَّهَاتُهُم جَالِسُونَ فِي مَخْضَرَة الْحَدِيْقَة وَيَتَحَادَثُون، بَعْضُ الأَطْفَال يَلْعَبُون بِالبَالُونَات.
The little girls are skipping ropes and some are running and trying to catch butterflies.	*waṭṭiflāt yaqfiznal ḥibāl wa ba'ḍuhunna yajrīna wa yuḥāwilnal imsāk bil farāsh.*	وَالطِّفْلاَت يَقْفِزْن الْحِبَال وَبَعْضُهُن يَجْرِيْن وَيُحَاوِلْن الإِمْسَاك بِالْفَرَاش.
Maryam: Is there any canteen in the park?	*Maryam: hal yūjad fil ḥadīqah maqṣaf?*	مَرْيَم: هَلْ يُوجَد فِي الْحَدِيْقَة مَقْصَف؟

Jamal: Yes, there is one. Do you want to have anything?	*Jamāl: nā'am, hunā maqṣaf hal turidīn an ta'khudhī shay'ā?*	جَمَال: نَعَم، هُنَا مَقْصَف. هَلْ تُرِيْدِيْن أَنْ تَأْخُذِي شَيْئاً؟
Maryam: Yes, I would like to take coffee.	*Maryam: nā'am urīd an ākhudh al qahwah.*	مَرْيَم: نَعَم، أُرِيْد أَنْ آخُذَ القَهْوَة.
Jamal: Ok dear, lets go to the canteen. We can get there cold drinks, fruit juice, sandwiches and ice-cream and, of course, your coffee too.	*Jamāl: ḥasanan yā ḥabībatī hayyā nadhhab ilal maqṣaf, sanajid hunāk al mashrūbāt al bāridah wa 'aṣīral fawākih was sandwishāt wal ais kirīm wa ṭab'an alqahwah laki.*	جَمَال: حَسَنًا يَا حَبِيْبَتِي هَيَّا نَذْهَب إِلَى الْمَقْصَف، سَنَجِدُ هُنَاك الْمَشْرُوبَات البَارِدَة وَعَصِيْرَ الْفَوَاكِه وَالسَّنْدوِشَات والأَيْس كِرِيْم وَطَبْعًا القَهْوَة لَك.
Jamal: And what would you like to have, Salma?	*Jamāl: wa mādhā tuḥibbīna an ta'khudhī yā Salmā?*	جَمَال: وَمَاذَا تُحِبِّيْن أَنْ تَأْخُذِى يَا سَلْمَى؟
Salma: Ice-cream, daddy.	*Salma: ais kirim yā abī.*	سَلْمَى: أَيْس كِرِيْم يَا أَبِي.
Jamal: What about you, Saeed?	*Jamāl: wa anta yā Sa'īd?*	جَمَال: وَأَنْتَ يَا سَعِيد؟
Saeed: Get me some potato chips and chocolates, daddy.	*Sa'īd: ishtari lī, yā abī, ruqāqāt baṭāṭiyyah wash shokolāt.*	سَعِيْد: اشْتَرِ لِي يَا أَبِي رُقَاقَات بَطَاطِيَّة والشُّوكُولات.
After the refreshment they all return home happily.	*wa ba'dat tafarruj kulluhum yarji'ūn ilal manzil fariḥīn.*	وَبَعْدَ التَّفَرُّج كُلُّهُم يَرْجِعُون إِلَى الْمَنْزِل فَرِحِيْن.

International Trade Fair

(al ma'riḍ at tijārī ad duwalī) الْمَعْرِض التِّجَارِي الدُّوَلِي

Saeed: Where would you like to go to this Sunday, dad?	*Sa'īd: aina turīd an tadhhab fī yaumil aḥad al qādim yā abī?*	سَعيد: أيْنَ تُرِيْد أنْ تَذْهَبَ فِي يَوْمِ الأحَد الْقَادِم يَا أبِي؟
Jamal: Don't you know my son, that the International Trade Fair is going to be held at the end of April?	*Jamāl: alā ta'rif yā bunayya annal ma'riḍ attijārī adduwalī sayabda' fī awākhiri shahri abrīl?*	جَمَال: ألاَ تَعْرِف يَا بُنَيَّ أنَّ الْمَعْرِض التِّجَارِي الدُّوَلِي سَيَبْدَأ فِي أوَاخِرِ شَهْرِ أبْرِيل؟
Saeed: Where will it be held, dad?	*Sa'īd: aina yan'aqidu hādhal ma'riḍ yā abī?*	سَعيد: أيْنَ يَنْعَقِدُ هَذَا الْمَعْرِض يَا أبِي؟
Jamal: It will be held on William Ground beside the Post Office Tower. This International Trade Fair is organized in this big ground in the month of April every year.	*Jamāl: hādhā yan'aqid fī maidāni wilyam bijiwār burj maktabil barīd. hādhal ma'riḍ yunaẓẓam kulla sanah fī hādhal maidān al wasī' bi kulli ihtimām wa naẓm fī shahri abrīl.*	جَمَال: هَذَا يَنْعَقِدُ فِي مَيْدَان وِلْيَم بِجِوَار بُرْج مَكْتَب الْبَرِيْد. هَذَا الْمَعْرِض يُنَظَّمُ كُلَّ سَنَة فِي هَذَا الْمَيْدَان الْوَسِيْع بِكُلِّ اهْتِمَام وَنَظْم فِي شَهْرِ أبْرِيْل.

Saeed: Is this a very big fair, dad?	*Sa'īd: hal hādhal ma'riḍ kabīr jiddā yā abī?*	سَعِيْد: هَلْ هَذَا الْمَعْرِض كَبِيْر جدًّا يَا أبِي؟
Jamal: Yes, my child. This fair has many big halls and each hall has so many pavilions.	*Jamāl: na'am yā bunaiya hādhal ma'riḍ yatakawwan min ṣālāt wa kullu ṣālah tata'allaf min ajniḥah kathīrah.*	جَمَال: نَعَم، يَا بُنَيّ. هَذَا الْمَعْرِض يَتَكَوَّن مِنْ صَالاَت، وَكُلُّ صَالَة تَتَألَّف مِنْ أَجْنِحَة كَثِيْرَة.
Saeed: Do the companies from the foreign countries also take part in it?	*Sa'īd: hal tushārik fīhi sharikāt minal bilād al ajnabiyyah aiḍan?*	سَعِيْد: هَلْ تُشَارِك فِيْه شَرِكَات مِنَ الْبِلاَدِ الأَجْنَبِيَّة أَيْضاً؟
Jamal: Yes, my child so many companies from all over the world take part in it. They purchase their stalls for the promotion of their different products.	*Jamāl: na'am yā bunayya tushārik fīhi sharikāt kathīrah min jamī'i anḥā'il 'ālam wa tuqīm fīhi ajniḥatahā litarwīji maṣnū'ātihā al mutanawwi'ah.*	جَمَال: نَعَم يَا بُنَيّ تُشَارِك فِيْه شَرِكَات كَثِيْرَة مِنْ جَمِيْعِ أَنْحَاء الْعَالَم وَتُقِيْم فِيْه أَجْنِحَتَهَا لِتَرْوِيْج مَصْنُوعَاتِهَا الْمُتَنَوِّعَة.
Every country has a separate pavilion: a pavilion for England, a pavilion for France, a pavilion for China, a pavilion for Germany, a pavilion for Japan, a pavilion for Switzerland and a pavilion for Saudia Arabia etc.	*hunāk janāḥ mukhaṣṣaṣ likulli balad, janāḥ li injaltarā wa janāḥ lil faransā wa janāḥ liṣṣīn wa janāḥ li almāniyā wa janāḥ lil yābān wa janāḥ li suwisrā wa janāḥ lil mamlikah as sa'ūdiyah al 'arabiyyah.*	هُنَاكَ جَنَاح مُخَصَّص لِكُلِّ بَلَد، جَنَاحٌ لإنْجَلْتَرا وَجَنَاح لِلْفَرَنسا وَجَنَاح لِلصِّيْن وَجَنَاح لأَلْمَانيا وَجَنَاح لِلْيَابَان وَجَنَاح لِسُوِيْسرا وَجَنَاح لِلْمَمْلَكَة السَّعُودِيَّة الْعَرَبِيَّة.
On Sunday next Jamal goes out with his family to visit the Fair.	*wa fī yaumil aḥad alqādim yakhruj Jamāl ma'a usratihi ilal ma'riḍ li mushāhadatih.*	وَفِي يَومِ الأَحَد الْقَادِم يَخْرُج جَمَال مَعَ أُسْرَتِه إلَى الْمَعْرِض لِمُشَاهَدَتِه.
The family reaches the fair at 10 a.m.	*waṣalatil usrah ilal ma'riḍ fis sā'ah al 'āshirah ṣabāḥan.*	وَصَلَت الأَسْرَة إِلَى الْمَعْرِض فِي السَّاعَة الْعَاشِرَة صَبَاحاً.

There is a great crowd inside and outside the ground.	*wa kāna hunāk izdiḥām kabīr fī dākhilil maidān wabi khārijihi.*	وَكَان هُنَاك ازْدِحَام كَبِير فِي دَاخِلِ الْمَيْدَان وَبخارجه.
Men, women and children all have come to see the fair. Some are standing at the ticket counter to purchase the tickets whereas some are waiting at the gate to enter.	*arrijāl wan nisā' wal aṭfāl kulluhum jā'ū limushāhadatil ma'riḍ, ba'ḍuhum yaqifūn 'alash shubbāk lishirā'it tadhākir wa ba'ḍuhum yantaẓirūnad dukhūl amāmal bāb.*	الرِّجَال وَالنِّسَاء والأطْفَال كُلُّهُم جَاءُوا لِمُشَاهَدَة الْمَعْرِض، بَعْضُهُم يَقِفُون عَلَى الشُّبَّاك لِشَرَاء التَّذَاكِر وَبَعْضُهُم يَنْتَظِرُونَ الدُّخُول أَمَامَ الْبَاب.
Jamāl purchases four tickets for his family and they all enter the exhibition ground.	*Jamāl yashtarī arba'a tadhākir li usratihi wa yadkhulūna maidānal ma'riḍ jamī'ā.*	جَمَال يَشْتَرِى أَرْبَع تَذَاكِر لِأُسْرَته وَيَدْخُلُون مَيْدَان الْمَعْرِض جَمِيْعاً.
At first they go to the hall which is full of clothes and other household things like carpets, blankets, pillows, curtains, bedsheets, furniture etc.	*hum yatawajjahūna awwalan ilā ṣālah mamlū'ah bil malābis wallawāzim al manziliyyah al ukhrā kassajjādāt wal baṭṭāniyyāt wal makhādd was sutur wal malāyāt wal athāth wa mā ilā dhālik.*	هُم يَتَوجَّهُون أَوَّلاً إِلَى صَالَة مَمْلُوءَة بِالْمَلَابِس وَاللَّوَازِم الْمَنْزِلِيَّة الأُخْرَى كَالسَّجَّادَات وَالْبَطَّانِيَات وَالْمَخَادّ وَالسُّتُر وَالْمَلَايَات وَالأَثَاث وَمَا إِلَى ذَلِك.
They get to see many kinds of clothes like readymade clothes, woven clothes, winter clothes; summer clothes etc.	*wa yūshāhidūn anwā'an kathīrah minal malābis kal malābis al jāhizah wa ghairil jāhizah, al malābis ash shitā'iyyah waṣ ṣaifiyyah wa mā ilā dhālik.*	وَيُشَاهِدُون أَنْوَاعاً كَثِيْرَةً مِن الْمَلَابِس كَالْمَلَابِس الْجَاهِزَة وَغَيْرِ الْجَاهِزَة، الْمَلَابِس الشِّتَائِيَّة وَالصَّيْفِيَّة وَمَا إِلَى ذَلِك.
The family after visiting most of the pavilions of this hall moves to the pavilion of China.	*ba'da mushāhadati akthari ajniḥati hādhihiṣ ṣālah tanṭaliqul usrah ilal janāḥ aṣ ṣīnī.*	بَعْد مُشَاهَدَة أَكْثَرِ أَجْنِحَة هَذه الصَّالَة تَنْطَلِقُ الأُسْرَة إِلَى الْجَنَاح الصِّيْنِي.

There they find many beautiful collections of pants and shirts, ties and hankerchiefs of varying colours.	*wa tajid fīhā majmu'āt jamīlah minal banṭlūnāt wal qumṣān war ribāṭāt wal manādīl min alwān mukhtalifah.*	وَتَجد فيْهَا مَجْمُوعَات جَميْلَة منَ الْبَنْطَلُونَات وَالْقُمْصَان وَالرِّبَاطَات وَالْمَنَاديْل منْ أَلْوَان مُخْتَلفَة.
They like the things so much that they ask about their prices.	*fatu'jibuhum hādhihil ashyā' fa'akhadhū yas'alūna 'an athmānihā.*	فَتُعْجِبُهُم هَذه الأشْيَاء فَأَخَذُوا يَسْأَلُون عَنْ أَثْمَانها.
Jamal: Hello! How much is this tie for?	*Jamāl: marḥabā mā thamanu hādhihir ribāṭah?*	جَمَال: مَرْحَبًا مَا ثَمَنُ هَذه الرِّبَاطَة؟
Salesman: Twenty pounds.	*al bā'i': 'ishrūna junaihan.*	الْبَائع: عشْرُونَ جُنَيْهاً.
Jamal: Any discount.	*Jamāl: ayya takhfīḍ?*	جَمَال: أيَّ تَخْفيْض؟
Salesman: This is after discount. Sir, its quality is good.	*al bā'i': na'am hādha ba'dat takhfīḍ. yā sayyidī hādhihi nau'uhā jayyid.*	الْبَائع: نَعَم، هَذَا بَعْدَ التَّخْفيْض. يَا سَيِّدي، هَذه نَوعُهَا جَيِّد.
Jamal: Please give me this.	*Jamāl: a'ṭinīhā min faḍlik.*	جَمَال: أعْطنيْهَا منْ فَضْلك.
Salesman: Thanks. And anything for this child?	*albā'i': shukran. wa ayyu shay' li hādhaṭ ṭifl?*	البَائع: شُكْراً، وَأيُّ شَيْء لهَذَا الطِّفْل؟
Maryam: Do you like anything, Saeed?	*Maryam: wa hal turīd shay'ā yā Sa'īd?*	مَريَم: وَهَل تُريْد شَيْئًا يَا سَعيْد؟
Saeed: Yes, I like this beautiful handkerchief.	*Sa'īd: na'am anā urīd hādhal mindīl al jamīl.*	سَعيد: نَعَم، أنَا أُريْد هَذَا الْمنْديل الْجَميل.
Maryam: Please give this handkerchief.	*Maryam: a'ṭinīhi min faḍlik.*	مَريَم: أعْطنيْه منْ فَضْلك.
The family comes out from this hall and moves to the hall which has toasters, grillers and ovens and	*takhrujul usrah min hādhihiṣ ṣālah wa tatawajjahu ilaṣ ṣālah allatī tujad fīhā al maḥāmiṣ*	تَخْرُج الأسْرَة منْ هَذه الصَّالَة وَتَتَوَجَّه إلَى الصَّالَة الَّتي تُوجَد فيْهَا الْمَحَامص وَالشَّوَّايَات

other things like plates, bowls, cups, spoons, knives and forks etc.	*wash shawwāyāt wal afrān wal ashyā' al ukhrā kal aṭbāq wal akwāb wal fanājīn wal malā'iq was sakākīn wash shaukāt wa naḥwahā.*	وَالأفْرَان وَالأشْيَاء الأخْرَى كَالأطْبَاق وَالأكْوَاب وَالْفَنَاجِيْن وَالْمَلاَعِق وَالسَّكَاكِين والشَّوكَات وَنَحْوَها.
After a while, they get tired and feel thirsty.	*wa ba'da qalīl yuṣībuhum atta'bu wal 'aṭashu.*	وَبَعْدَ قَلِيْل يُصِيْبُهُم التَّعَب والْعَطَش.
They go to a canteen and take some snacks and soft drinks.	*hum yadhhabūn ilā maqṣaf wa yatanāwalūn alwajbāt alkhafīfah wal mashrūbāt al ghāziyah.*	هُمْ يَذْهَبُون إِلَى مَقْصَف وَيَتَنَاوَلُون الوَجْبَات الْخَفِيْفَة والْمَشْرُوبَات الْغَازِيَة.
And after resting for a while, they go to the hall which has electrical goods.	*wa ba'da istirāḥah qalīlah yatawajjahūn ilā ṣālatil baḍā'i' al kahrabā'iyyah.*	وَبَعْدَ اسْتِرَاحَة قَلِيْلَة يَتَوَجَّهُون إِلَى صَالَة الْبَضَائِع الكَهْرَبَائِيَّة.
There they see washing machines, heaters, irons, refrigerators, deep freezers, air-conditioners, air-coolers and vacuum cleaners manufactured by different companies from Asia, Europe and America.	*wa yushāhidūna hunāk al ghassālāt was sakhkhānāt wal makāwī wath thallājāt wal mujammidāt wal mukayyifāt wal mubarridāt wal makānis al kahrabā'iyyah min sharikāt mukhtalifah min āsiyā wa aurubbā wa amrīkā.*	وَيُشَاهِدُون هُنَاكَ الغَسَّالاَت وَالسَّخَّانَات وَالْمَكَاوِى وَالثَّلاَّجَات وَالْمُجَمِّدَات والْمُكَيِّفَات وَالْمُبَرِّدَات وَالْمَكَانِس الْكَهْرَبَائِيَّة مِنْ شَرِكَات مُخْتَلِفَة مِنْ آسِيَا وَأَوْرُبا وَأَمْرِيْكَا.
At last they head towards the hall which has computers, T.V., VDO, mobile phones, cassettes, taperecords, cameras and watches of	*wa akhīran yatawajjahūn ilaṣ ṣālah allatī yujad fīhā alkambiutar wat tilfiziyūn wal fidīyu wal hawātif al jawwālah wash*	وَأخيْراً يَتَوجَّهُون إِلَى الصَّالَة الَّتِي يُوجَد فِيْهَا الكَمْبِيُوتَر وَالتِّلفِزْيُون وَالفِيْدِيو وَالْهَوَاتِف الْجَوَّالَة وَالشَّرِيْطَات وَالْمُسَجِّلاَت

exquisite designs.	*sharīṭāt wal musajjilāt wal kāmīrāt wal sā'āt min ṭirāz mumtāz.*	وَالكَامِيْرَات وَالسَّاعَات مِن طِرَاز مُمْتَاز.
After visiting this hall Jamal comes out of the exhibition ground with his family and they go back home.	*wa ba'da mushāhadati hādhihiṣ ṣālah Jamāl yakhruj min maidānil ma'riḍ ma'a usratih wa yarji'ūn ilal manzil.*	وَبَعْدَ مُشَاهدَة هَذه الصَّالَة جَمَال يَخْرُج مِن مَيْدَان الْمَعْرِض مَعَ أسْرَته وَيَرجِعُونَ إلَى الْمَنْــزِل.

At a Chemist Shop
(fī ṣaidaliyyah) فِي صَيْدَلِيَّة

Jamal is ill. His father, Fauzan, calls a doctor, who prescribes some medicines.	*Jamāl marīḍ fayaṭlub abūhu Fauzān ṭabīban, huwa yaṣifu lahu ba'ḍal adwiyah.*	جَمَال مَرِيْضٌ فَيَطْلُب أبُوه فَوزَان طَبِيْباً، هُوَ يَصِف لَه بَعْضَ الأَدْوِيَة.
Fauzan's younger son Nasir goes to a chemist shop located at the William Street to purchase the medicines prescribed by the doctor.	*yadhhab ibnu fauzān al aṣghar Nāṣir ilā ṣaidaliyah wāqi'ah fi shāri' wilyam li shirā'il adwiyah allatī waṣafahaṭ ṭabīb.*	يَذْهَبُ ابْنُ فَوزَان الأصْغَر نَاصِر إلَى صَيْدَلِيَّة وَاقِعَة فِي شَارِع وِلْيَم لِشِرَاء الأَدْوِيَة الَّتِي وَصَفَهَا الطَّبِيْب.
Nasir meets Salim on the way.	*yalqā Nāṣir Sāliman fiṭ ṭarīq.*	يَلْقَى نَاصِر سَالِمًا فِي الطَّرِيق.
Salim: Where are you going, Nasir?	*Sālim: ilā aina dhāhib anta yā Nāṣir?*	سَالِم: إلَى أيْنَ ذَاهِب أنْتَ يَا نَاصِر؟
Nasir: To a chemist shop.	*Nāṣir: ilaṣ ṣaidaliyah.*	نَاصِر: إلَى الصَّيْدَلِيَّة.
Salim: Why?	*Sālim: limah?*	سَالِم: لِمَه؟

Nasir: My elder brother Jamal is ill for a few days.	*Nāṣir: akhil kabīr Jamāl marīḍ mundhu ayyām.*	نَاصِر: أخِي الْكَبِيْر جَمَال مَرِيْض مُنْذُ أيَّام.
Salim: Did he see any doctor?	*Sālim: hal zāra ṭabīban?*	سَالِم: هَلْ زَارَ طَبِيْباً؟
Nasir: Yes, he did and the doctor has prescribed some medicines for him.	*Nāṣir: na'am, wa qad waṣafa lahuṭ ṭabību ba'ḍal adwiyah.*	نَاصِر: نَعَم، وَقَد وَصَفَ لَه الطَّبِيْبُ بَعْضَ الأدْوِيَة.
Salim: Which disease is he suffering from?	*Sālim: bi ayyi dā' muṣāb huwa?*	سَالِم: بِأيِّ دَاء مُصَاب هُو؟
The doctor says that he is suffering from typhoid.	*Ṇāsir: huwa muṣāb bil ḥummā at tīfiyyah kamā yaqūluṭ ṭabīb.*	نَاصِر: هُو مُصَاب بِالْحُمَّى التِّيفِيَّة كَمَا يَقُولُ الطَّبِيْب.
He has accute pain in his stomach.	*wa huwa yash'ur bi alam shadīd fil ma'idah.*	وَهُو يَشْعُر بِأَلَم شَدِيْد فِي الْمَعدَة.
Salim: Which shop are you going to purchase your medicines?	*Sālim: min ayyi ṣaidaliyah turīd an tashtariya hāḍhihil adwiyah?*	سَالِم: مِن أيِّ صَيْدَلِيَّة تُرِيْد أنْ تَشْتَرِى هَذِه الأدْوِيَة؟
Nasir: The one located at the William Street.	*Nāṣir: minaṣ ṣaidaliyah allatī taqa' fi shāri' wilyam.*	نَاصِر: مِنَ الصَّيْدَلِيَّة الَّتِي تَقَع فِي شَارِع وِلْيَم.
Salim: Is this a big chemist shop?	*Sālim: hal hādhihi ṣaidaliyah kabīrah?*	سَالِم: هَل هَذِه صَيْدَلِيَّة كَبِيْرَة؟
Nasir: Yes, and it is famous too.	*Nāṣir: na'am, wa hādhihi shahīrah aiḍan.*	نَاصِر: نَعَم، وَهَذِه شَهِيْرَة أيْضاً.
It has both modern and traditional medicines.	*wa tūjad fīhā al adwiyah al ḥadīthah wat taqlīdiyyah.*	وَتُوجَد فِيْهَا الأدْوِيَة الْحَدِيْثَة وَالتَّقْلِيْدِيَّة.
They enter the chemist shop.	*hum yadkhulūnaṣ ṣaidaliyah.*	هُم يَدْخُلُون الصَّيْدَلِيَّة.
Chemist: What do you want?	*aṣṣaidalī: mādhā turīd?*	الصَّيْدَلِي: مَاذَا تُرِيْد؟
Nasir: I want to purchase some medicines.	*Nāṣir: urīd an ashtariya ba'ḍal adwiyah.*	نَاصِر: أُرِيْد أنْ اَشْتَرِى بَعْضَ الأدْوِيَة.

Chemist: Where is the prescription?	*aṣṣaidalī: ainal waṣfah?*	الصَّيْدَلِي: أيْنَ الوَصْفَة؟
Nasir: Here it is.	*Nāṣir: hādhihi hiya.*	نَاصِر: هَذه هيَ.
Chemist to the keeper: Bring that blue box and that syrup too.	*aṣṣaidalī lil'āmil: hāti tilkal 'ulbah azzarqā' wa dhālikash sharāb aiḍā.*	الصَّيْدَلِي لِلْعَامِل: هَات تِلْكَ العُلْبَة الزَّرْقَاء وَذَلك الشَّرَاب أيْضاً.
Chemist to Nasir: Here are your medicines.	*aṣṣaidalī li Nāṣir: khudhil adwiyah.*	الصَّيْدَلِي لِنَاصِر: خُذ الأدْوِيَة.
Nasir: Can you tell me please how it should be taken?	*Nāṣir: hal tuwaḍḍiḥ kaifa yutanāwal min faḍlik?*	نَاصِر: هَلْ تُوَضِّح كَيْفَ يُتَنَاول منْ فَضْلك؟
Chemist: Yes, sure. This box contains blue pills. Take two pills after lunch and two after dinner and two spoonfuls from this syrup before the breakfast and only one capsule before going to bed.	*aṣṣaidalī: ay na'am, fī hādhihil 'ulbah ḥubūb zarqā' ta'khudh ḥabbain ba'dal ghadā' wa habbain ba'dal 'ashā' wa mil'aqatain min hādhash sharāb qablal fuṭūr wa kabsūlah faqaṭ qablan naum.*	الصَّيْدَلِي: أيْ نَعَم، فِي هَذه العُلْبَة حُبُوب زَرْقَاء تَأخُذ حَبَّيْن بَعْدَ الْغَدَاء وَحَبَّيْن بَعْد الْعشَاء وَملْعَقَتَين منْ هَذَا الشَّرَاب قَبْل الْفُطُور وَكَبْسُولَة فَقَط قَبْل النَّوم.
Nasir: With hot water or ordinary water?	*Nāṣir: bil mā'is sākhin am bil mā'il 'ādī?*	نَاصِر: بالْمَاء السَّاخِن أم بالْمَاء العَادي؟
Chemist? With ordinary water.	*aṣṣaidalī: bil mā'il 'ādī.*	الصَّيْدَلِي: بالْمَاء الْعَادي.
Nasir: How much do I have to pay for this?	*Nāṣir: kam adfa' lidhālik?*	نَاصِر: كَمْ أدْفَع لِذَلك؟
Chemist: Fifty pounds	*aṣṣaidalī: khamsīna junaihan.*	الصَّيْدَلِي: خَمْسِين جُنَيهاً.
Nasir: Thanks:	*Nāṣir: shukran*	نَاصِر: شُكراً
Chemist: I wish your brother an early recovery.	*aṣṣaidalī: atamannā li akhīka shifā'an 'ājilan.*	الصَّيْدَلِي: أتَمَنَّى لأخِيْك شفَاءً عَاجلاً.
Nasir: Thank you.	*Nāṣir: shukran.*	نَاصِر: شُكْراً.

At the Railway Station

(*fī maḥaṭṭatil qiṭār*) فِي مَحَطَّة الْقِطَار

Jamal never travelled by a train. This time he wanted to travel to London by a train with his family.	*Jamāl lam yusāfir bil qiṭār qaṭṭ fa arāda hādhihil marrah an yusāfir ilā landan bil qiṭār ma'a usratih.*	جَمَال لَم يُسَافِر بِالْقِطَار قَطّ فَأَرَادَ هَذِه الْمَرَّة أَن يُسَافِر إِلَى لَنْدن بِالْقِطَار مَعَ أسْرَته.
He hired a taxi for Sirsakeford Station. He and his family got in the taxi.	*fasta'jara tāksī limaḥaṭṭah sarsīkford wa rakibahu ma'a usratih.*	فَاسْتَأْجَرَ تَاكْسِي لِمَحَطَّة سَرسِيكفُورد وَرَكِبَه مَع أُسْرَته.
His friend Nasir was also with them.	*wa kāna ma'ahum ṣadīquhu Nāṣir aiḍan.*	وَكَانَ مَعَهُم صَدِيْقُه نَاصِر أيْضاً.
He was going to the station to see them off.	*kāna yadhhab ilal maḥaṭṭah litaudī'ihim.*	كَانَ يَذْهَب إِلَى الْمَحَطَّة لِتَودِيْعِهِم.
Sirsakeford is a big railway station and always full of the passengers.	*sirsīkford maḥaṭṭah kabīrah wa muzdaḥimah bil musāfirīna dā'imā.*	سَرسِيكفُورد مَحَطَّة كَبِيْرَة وَمُزْدَحِمَة بِالْمُسَافِرِين دَائِمًا.
After arriving at the station Jamal rushed to the enquiry counter.	*ba'dal wuṣūl ilal maḥaṭṭah asra'a Jamāl ilā shubbākil isti'lām.*	بَعْدَ الْوُصُول إِلَى الْمَحَطَّة أَسْرَعَ جَمَال إِلَى شُبَّاك الاسْتِعْلَام.

The following dialogue took place between him and the man at the enquiry counter.	*wa dāra bainahu wa baina muwaẓẓafil isti'lāmāt hādhal ḥiwār.*	وَدَارَ بَيْنَه وَبَيْن مُوَظَّف الاستِعْلاَمَات هَذَا الحِوَار.
Jamal: Good morning.	*Jamāl: ṣabāḥal khair.*	جَمَال: صَبَاحَ الْخَيْر
Employee: Good morning. What can I do for you, sir?	*al muwaẓẓaf: ṣabāḥan nūr ayya khidmah yā sayyidī?*	الْمُوَظَّف: صَبَاح النُّور. أيّ خدْمَة يَا سَيِّدي؟
Jamal: I want to go to London.	*Jamāl: urīdudh dhahāb ilā landan.*	جَمَال: أرِيْدُ الذَّهَاب إلَى لَندَن.
Employee: When do you want to travel?	*al muwaẓẓaf: matā turīd an tusāfir?*	الْمُوَظَّف: مَتَى تُرِيْد أنْ تُسَافِر؟
Jamal: Today.	*Jamāl: al yaum*	جَمَال: الْيَوم
Employee: By which train would you like to travel?	*al muwaẓẓaf: bi ayyi qiṭār turīd an tusāfir?*	الْمُوَظَّف: بِأيّ قِطَار تُرِيْد أنْ تُسَافِر؟
There are both ordinary trains and express trains going to London.	*hunāk qiṭār 'ādī wa qiṭār sarī' dhāhib ilā landan.*	هُنَاك قِطَار عَادي وَقِطَار سَرِيْع ذَاهِب إلَى لَنْدَن.
Jamal: By express train.	*Jamāl: bi qiṭār sarī'.*	جَمَال: بِقِطَار سَرِيع.
Employee: O.K. There is London Express today, which goes to London.	*al muwaẓẓaf: ḥasanan fa hunāk landan eksbres al yaum, hādhā yadhhab ilā landan.*	الْمُوَظَّف: حَسَنًا، فَهُنَاك لَنْدَن ايْكسبَرِيس اليَوْم، هَذَا يَذْهَب إلَى لَندن.
The journey in it will be very comfortable.	*yakūnus safar fīhi murīḥan jiddā.*	يَكُون السَّفَر فِيْه مُرِيحًا جدًّا.
It will take only eight hours.	*hādhā ya'khudh thamānī sā'āt faqaṭ.*	هَذَا يَأخُذُ ثَمَانِي سَاعَات فَقَط.
It leaves Sirsakeford at 10 a.m. and arrives London at 6 p.m.	*hādhal qiṭār yughādir sarsīkford fis sā'atil 'āshirah ṣabāḥan wa yaṣilu ilā landan fis sā'atis sādisah masā'an.*	هَذَا القِطَار يُغَادِر سِرسيكفورد فِي السَّاعَة العَاشِرَة صَبَاحًا وَيَصِل إلَى لَنْدَن فِي السَّاعَة السَّادِسَة مَسَاء.

Jamal: Is it an air conditioned train?	*Jamāl: hal hādhal qiṭār mukayyaf bil hawā'?*	جَمَال: هَل هَذَا القِطَار مَكَيَّف بِالْهَوَاء؟
Employee: Yes, sir.	*al muwaẓẓaf: na'am, yā sayyidī.*	الْمُوَظَّف: نَعَم، يَا سَيِّدِي.
Other facilities are also available there like delicious meals and complementary soft drinks.	*wa tatawaffar fīhi at tashīlāt al ukhrā aiḍan amthāl al wajbāt al ladhīdhah wal mashrūbāt al ghāziyah al mutatāmmah.*	وَتَتَوفَّر فِيْه التَّسْهِيلاَت الأخْرَى أيْضاً أمْثَال الْوَجْبَات اللَّذِيْذَة وَالْمَشْرُوبَات الغَازِيَة الْمُتَتَامَّة.
Jamal: Thank you. Where can I get the tickets?	*Jamāl: shukran. fa min aina yumkinunī an ashtariyat tadhākir?*	جَمَال: شُكْراً. فَمِن أيْنَ يُمْكِنُنِي أن اَشْتَرِي التَّذَاكِر؟
Employee: For that you will have to go to the reservation office.	*al muwaẓẓaf: idhhab lidhālik ilā maktabil ḥajz.*	الْمُوَظَّف: اذْهَب لِذَلِك إلَى مَكْتَب الْحَجْز.
Jamal: Where is the reservation office?	*Jamāl: 'aina maktabul ḥajz?*	جَمَال: أيْنَ مَكْتَب الْحَجْز؟
Employee: Beside the William Hotel.	*al muwaẓẓaf: bi jiwāri funduq wilyam.*	الْمُوَظَّف: بِجِوَار فُنْدُق وِلْيَم.

Reservation Office

(maktabul ḥajz) مَكْتَبُ الْحَجْز

Jamal rushes to the reservation office. This is a very large hall. There are many counters and in front of each counter there is a long queue.	*Jamāl yusri' ilā maktabil ḥajz hādhihi ṣālah kabīrah jiddā wa hunāka shabābīk kathīrah wa amāma kulli shubbāk ṭābūr ṭawīl.*	جَمَال يُسْرِع إلَى مَكْتَب الْحَجْز. هَذه صَالَةُ كَبِيْرَة جدّا. وَهُنَاك شَبَابِيْك كَثِيْرَة وَأمَامَ كُلِّ شُبَّاك طَابُور طَوِيْل.
Jamal stands on a queue in front of the first class counter.	*Jamāl yaqif fī ṭābūr amāma shubbāk litadhākirid darajatil ūlā.*	جَمَال يَقِف فِي طَابُور أمَام شُبَّاك لِتَذَاكِر الدَّرَجَة الأوْلَى.

Jamal: I would like to have four tickets for London.	*Jamāl: urīd an 'ākhudh arba'a tadhākir li landan.*	جَمَال: أُرِيْدُ أنْ آخُذَ أرْبَع تَذَاكِر لِلندن.
Employee: For which class?	*al muwazzaf: li ayyi darajah?*	الْمُوَظَّف: لأيِّ دَرَجَة؟
Jamal: For the first class.	*Jamāl: lid darajatil ūlā.*	جَمَال: للدَّرَجَة الأولَى.
Employee: All the berths in it have already been reserved.	*al muwazzaf: kullul maqā'id fīhā qad ḥujizat min qabl.*	الْمُوَظَّف: كُلُّ الْمَقَاعِد فِيْهَا قَد حُجِزَت مِن قَبْل.
Do you like in the upper class?	*hal turīd bid darajatil 'āliyah?*	هَل تُرِيد بِالدَّرَجَة الْعَالِيَة؟
Jamal: Yes.	*Jamāl: na'am.*	جَمَال: نَعَم.
Jamal: How many pounds do I have to pay for this?	*Jamāl: kam junaihan uwaddī li dhālik?*	جَمَال: كَمْ جُنَيْهًا أُوَدِّي لِذَلك؟
Employee: One hundred pounds.	*al muwazzaf: mi'ata junaihin.*	اَلْمُوَظَّف: مِأةَ جُنَيه.
Jamal: Thank you.	*Jamāl: shukran.*	جَمَال: شُكْراً.

Conversation with the Porter

(al muḥādathah ma'ash shayyāl) الْمُحَادَثَة مَعَ الشَّيَّال

Nasir: Porter!	*Nāsir: yā shayyāl!*	نَاصِر: يَا شَيَّال!
Porter: At your service sir.	*shayyāl: ḥāḍir fī khidmatikum yā sayyidī.*	شَيَّال: حَاضِر فِي خِدْمَتِكُم يَا سَيِّدي.
Nasir: Could you please carry this suitcase and this box?	*Nāṣir: hal taḥmil hādhihish shanṭah wa hādhaṣ ṣundūq min faḍlik?*	نَاصِر: هَلْ تَحْمل هَذه الْشَّنْطَة وَهَذَا الصُّنْدُوق مِن فَضْلك؟
The train has arrived at the platform and it will depart in a few minutes.	*innal qiṭār qad waṣala ilar raṣīf wa innahu sayughādir al maḥaṭṭah fī thawānin.*	إنَّ الْقِطَار قَد وَصَل إلَى الرَّصِيف وَإنَّه سَيُغَادِر الْمَحَطَّة فِي ثَوَان.

Porter: To which platform?	*shayyāl: ilā ayyi raṣīf?*	شيال: إلَى أيِّ رَصِيْف؟
Nasir: To platform No 12.	*Nāṣir: ilā raṣīf raqm ithnā 'ashara.*	نَاصِر: إلَى رَصِيْف رَقم ١٢
Jamal: Did you purchase platform ticket, friend?	*Jamāl: hal ishtaraita tadhkiratar rasīf yā ṣadīqī?*	جَمَال: هَلْ اشْتَرَيْتَ تَذْكَرَة الرَّصِيْف يَا صَدِيْقِي؟
Nasir: No, I didn't.	*Nāṣir: lā, lam ashtari.*	نَاصِر: لاَ، لَمْ اَشْتَرِ.
Jamal: Hurry up, brother!	*Jamāl: fa 'asri' yā akhī.*	جَمَال: فَأَسْرِع يَا أَخِي.
Nasir: Porter! Wait for a minute.	*Nāṣir: yā shayyāl intaẓir laḥẓah.*	نَاصِر: يَا شَيَّال اِنْتَظِر لَحْظَةً
Porter: yes, sir.	*shayyāl: na'am yā sayyidī.*	شَيَّال: نَعَم، يَا سَيِّدِي.
Now they all are at the platform. The platform is full of people.	*al ān kulluhum 'alar raṣīf warraṣīf mamlū' bin nās.*	الآن كُلُّهُم عَلَى الرَّصِيْف وَالرَّصِيْف مَمْلُوء بِالنَّاس.
Some of them are getting in the train whereas some others are getting down from it.	*ba'ḍuhum yarkabūnal qiṭār wa ba'ḍuhum yanzilūna minhu.*	بَعْضُهُم يَركَبُون القِطَار وَبَعْضُهُم يَنْزِلُون مِنْه.
Some are waiting for their relatives who are to come. Some of the people there have come to see off their friends.	*wa ba'ḍuhum yantaẓirūna aqribā'ahum al qādimīn wa ba'ḍuhum qad jā'ū li taudī'i aṣdiqā'ihim.*	وَبَعْضُهُم يَنْتَظِرُون أقْرِبَاءَهُم الْقَادِمِيْنَ وَبَعْضُهُم قَدْ جَاءُوا لِتَودِيْع أَصْدِقَاءِهِم.
Jamal and his family get in the train and thanks his friend Nasir.	*yarkab Jamāl al qiṭār ma'a usratih wa yashkur liṣadīqih Nāṣir.*	يَرْكَب جَمَال الْقِطَار مَعَ أُسْرَتِه وَيَشْكُر لِصَدِيْقِه نَاصِر.
Nasir wishes them a happy journey.	*Nāṣir yatmannā lahum riḥlatan sa'īdah.*	نَاصِر يَتَمَنَّى لَهُم رِحْلَةً سَعِيْدَة.

Visiting a Friend

(ziyāratu ṣadīq) زِيَارَةُ صَدِيْق

Jamal received a telegraph from his friend Khalid, who invited Jamal and his family to a party he wanted to throw at his house on the occasion of his son's success in the Annual Examination.	*tasallama Jamāl tilighrāfan min ṣadīqihi Kālid alladhī da'āhu ma'a 'ā'ilatihi ilā ma'dubah yurīd an yuqīmahā fī manzilihi bimunāsabatī najāḥibnihi fil ikhtibār assanawī.*	تَسَلَّمَ جَمَال تِلْغِرَافًا مِن صَـــدِيْقه خَالد الَّذي دَعَاه مَعَ عَائِلَته إِلَى مَأدُبَة يُرِيْد أن يُقِيْمَهَا فِي مَنْزِله بِمُنَاسَبَة نَجَاح ابْنِه فِي الاخْتِبَار السَّنَوِي.
Jamal informs his wife Maryam about this.	*Jamāl yukhbir zaujatahu Maryam bihādhā.*	جَمَال يُخْبِر زَوجَته مريَم بِهذَا.
Jamal: would you like to attend the party?	*Jamāl: hal tuḥibbīn an taḥḍuril ma'dubah?*	جَمَال: هَل تُحِبِّيْن أَنْ تَحْضُرِى الْمَأْدُبَة؟
Maryam: Yes, with great pleasure.	*Maryam: na'am bikulli surūr.*	مَرِيَم: نَعَم، بِكُلِّ سُرُور.
Jamal: We must buy some presents for them.	*Jamāl: yajib an nashtarīya ba'ḍat taḥā'if lahum.*	جَمَال: يَجِب أن نَشْتَرى بَعْض التَّحَائِف لَهُم.

Maryam: Yes, we will buy some sweets and a nice suit for the boy.	*Maryam: na'am, nashtarī ba'ḍal ḥalāwā wa badhlah anīqah lilwalad.*	مَريَم: نَعَم، نَشتَرى بَعْضَ الْحَلاوَى وَبَذْلَة أنِيقَة لِلْوَلَد.
Jamal: Yes, that will be good.	*Jamāl: na'am hādhā yakūn jayyidā.*	جَمَال: نَعَم، هَذَا يَكُون جَيِّداً.
Jamal, with his wife, went to the market and bought some sweets and a suit for the boy.	*dhahaba Jamāl ma'a zaujatihi ilas sūq washtarā ba'ḍal ḥalāwā wa badhlah lilwalad.*	ذَهَب جَمَال مَعَ زَوجَته إلَى السُّوق وَاشتَرَى بَعْضَ الْحَلاوَى وَ بَذْلَة لِلْوَلَد.
Then they headed for khalid's home.	*thumman ṭalaqū ilā manzili Kalid.*	ثُمَّ انْطَلَقُوا إلَى مَنزِل خَالِد.
His friend khalid was already present at home.	*kāna ṣadīquhu Khālid ḥāḍiran fil manzil.*	كَانَ صَدِيقُه خَالِد حَاضِراً فِي الْمَنْزِل.
He received the family warmly.	*huwa istaqbalal usrah bi ḥarārah.*	هُوَ اسْتَقْبَلَ الأُسْرَة بِحَرارَة.
Khalid: How are you, friend?	*Khālid: kaifal ḥāl yā ṣadīqī?*	خَالد: كَيْفَ الْحَال يَاصَدِيقِي؟
Jamal: Fine, thank you. And you?	*Jamāl: ṭayyib, shukran, wa antum?*	جَمَال: طَيِّب، شُكْراً. وَأنتُم؟
Khalid: Very well.	*Khalid: bikhair wa 'āfiyah.*	خَالد: بِخَيْر وَعَافِيَة.
Jamal: We are happy to know about your son's success at exams.	*Jamāl: kunnā fariḥnā jiddan binajāḥi ibnika fil ikhtibār.*	جَمَال: كُنَّا فَرِحْنَا جـــدًّا بِنَجَاحِ ابْنِك فِي الاخْتِبَار.
Where is that intelligent boy?	*aina dhālikal walad adhdhakī?*	أيْنَ ذَلِك الْوَلَد الذَّكِي؟
Khalid: He has gone to the market with his mom.	*Khālid: huwa dhahaba ilas sūq ma'a ummihi.*	خَالد: هُوَ ذَهَب إلَى السُّوقِ مَعَ أُمِّه.
They will be back in a few minutes.	*innahum yarji'ūn ba'da daqā'iq.*	إنَّهُم يَرْجِعُون بَعْدَ دَقَائِق.
Many other guests were also present there.	*Kāna kathīrum minaḍ ḍuyūf maujūdīn aiḍan hunāk.*	كَانَ كَثِيرٌ مِنَ الضُّيُوف مَوجُودِين أيْضاً هُنَاك.

They were all seated in the drawing room and talking to each other.	*wa kāna kulluhum jālisīna fī ghurfatil julūs wa yataḥādathūn.*	وَكَانَ كُلُّهُم جَالسِيْن فِي غُرْفَة الْجُلُوس وَيَتَحَادَثُون.
Soon, Khalid's little son Faisal enters the room quickly.	*Faiṣal ibnu Khālid aṣṣaghīr yadkhulul ghurfah sar'āna.*	فَيْصَل ابْنُ خَالد الصَّغير يَدخُل الغُرْفَة سَرعَان.
Faisal: Hello uncle!	*Faiṣal: ālū 'amm!*	فَيصَل: آلو عَمّ!
Jamal: Hello Faisal! How are you?	*Jamāl: ālū Faiṣal! kaifa ḥāluk?*	جَمَال: آلو فَيْصَل! كَيْفَ حَالُك؟
Faisal: Fine uncle, thank you.	*Faiṣal: bikhair yā 'amm, shukran.*	فَيْصَل: بِخَيْر يَا عَمّ، شُكْراً.
Jamal: congratulations on your success.	*Jamāl: tahni'āt 'alā najāḥik.*	جَمَال: تَهْنِئَات عَلَى نَجَاحك.
Faisal: Thank you.	*Faiṣal: shukran.*	فَيْصَل: شُكراً.
Khalid brings cold drink and juice to them.	*yuqaddimu Khālid al mashrūbāt al bāridah wal 'aṣīr ilaihim.*	يُقدِّم خَالد الْمَشْرُوبَات الْبَاردَة وَالعَصِيْر إِلَيْهِم.
Jamal takes cold drink and his wife takes mango juice.	*Jamāl ya'khudhu al mashrūb al bārid wa ta'khudh zaujatuhu 'aṣīra manjā.*	جَمَال يَأخُذُ الْمَشْرُوب الْبَارِد وَ تَأخُذُ زَوْجَتُه عَصِيْرَمَنْجَا.
After that Jamal and other guests have a sumptuous lunch.	*wa ba'da dhālik yatanāwalu Jamāl waḍ ḍuyūf al ākharūn al ghadā' as sakhī.*	وَبَعْد ذَلك يَتَنَاوَلُ جَمَال وَالضُّيُوف الآخَرُون الْغَدَاء السَّخِي.
After lunch everyone asked permission to leave.	*wa ba'dal ghadā' ista'dhana kullu wāḥidim minhum lilmughādarah.*	وَبَعْدَ الْغَدَاء اسْتَأذَنَ كُلُّ وَاحِدٍ مِنهُم لِلْمُغَادَرَة.
They all enjoyed Khalid's hospitality.	*kulluhum tamatta'ū bi ḍiyāfati Khālid.*	كُلُّهُم تَمَتَّعُوا بِضِيَافَة خَالِد.
Jamal: Thanks for the invitation.	*Jamāl: shukran lidda'wah*	جَمَال: شُكراً لِلدَّعْوة.
Khalid: Not at all.	*Khālid: 'afwan.*	خَالِد: عَفواً.

Sightseeing

(ziyāratul āthār al qadīmah) زِيَارَةُ الآثَار القَدِيْمَة

Faisal: What should we do this evening, Fahad?	*Faiṣal: mādhā naf'al hādhal masā' yā Fahad?*	فَيصَل: مَاذَا نَفْعَل هَذَا الْمَسَاء يَا فَهْد؟
Fahad: I've an idea. We should go and see some of the ancient momuments.	*Fahad: 'indī fikrah. linadhhab wa nushāhid ba'ḍal āthār al qadīmah.*	فَهْد: عِنْدِي فِكْرَة. لِنَذْهَب وَ نُشَاهِد بَعْضَ الآثَار الْقَدِيْمَة.
Faisal: Yes, and what do you want to see?	*Faiṣal: na'am, wa mādhā turīd an tushāhid?*	فَيصَل: نَعَم، وَمَاذَا تُرِيْد أن تُشَاهِد؟
Fahad: Have you ever visited the Pyramids and the Sphinx?	*Fahad: hal sabaqa laka an shāhadtal ahrām wa abul haul?*	فَهْد: هَل سَبَق لَكَ أن شَاهَدْتَ الأهْرَام وَأبوالْهَول؟
Faisal: No, friend.	*Faiṣal: lā yā ṣadīqī.*	فَيصَل: لاَ، يَا صَدِيْقِي.
Fahad: Come with me. We'll go and see the Pyramids and the Sphinx.	*Fahad: ta'āl ma'ī nadhhab wa nushāhidil ahrām wa abul haul.*	فَهْد: تَعَال مَعِي نَذْهَب وَنُشَاهِد الأهْرَام وَأبوالْهَول.
We would also take some photographs of	*wa na'khudh hunāka ba'ḍa ṣuwari hādhihil*	وَ نَأخُذ هُنَاك بَعْضَ صُوَر

these marvellous monuments.	*'āthār al 'ajībah aiḍan.*	هٰذه الآثَار الْعَجِيْبَة أيضاً.
Faisal: have you got any camera?	*Faiṣal: hal ma'ak kāmīrā?*	فَيصَل: هَل مَعَك كَاميْرا؟
Fahad: Yes, I've got a good quality camera.	*Fahad: na'am, ma'ī kāmīrā min nau' mumtāz.*	فَهْد: نَعم، مَعِي كَاميْرا مِن نَوع مُمْتَاز.
Fahad: Do you know what this statue is?	*Fahad: hal ta'rif mā hādhat timthāl?*	فَهْد: هَل تَعْرف مَا هٰذَا التِّمْثَال؟
Faisal: No, friend. Did you ever tell me about it?	*Faiṣal: lā yā ṣadīqī. hal akhbartanī 'anhu qablu?*	فَيصَل: لاَ يَا صَدِيْقِي. هَل أخبَرْتَني عَنه قَبْل؟
Fahad: This is the Sphinx, one of the statues of Ancient Egypt.	*Fahad: hādhā huwa abul haul timthāl min tamāthīlil miṣr al qadīmah.*	فَهْد: هٰذَا هُوَ أبوالْهَول، تمثَال مِنْ تَمَاثِيْل الْمِصْر الْقَدِيْمَة.
Faisal: This is a strange statue. It's head is that of a human whereas his body is that of an animal.	*Faiṣal: hādhā timthāl 'ajīb ra'suhu ra'sul insān wa jismuhu jismul ḥaiwān.*	فَيصَل: هٰذَا تمثَال عَجِيْب، رَأسُهُ رَأسُ الإنْسَان وَجِسْمُه جِسْمُ الْحَيْوَان.
I've seen many statues but never one like this.	*shāhattu tamāthīl kathīrah walākin lam ushāhid mithla hādhat timthāl qaṭṭ.*	شَاهَدتُ تَمَاثِيل كَثِيْرة وَلَكِن لَم أُشَاهِد مِثْل هٰذَا التِّمْثَال قَطّ.
For how long this statue has been here?	*mundhu matā hādhat timthāl qā'im hunā?*	مُنْذ مَتى هٰذَا التِّمْثَال قَائِم هُنَا؟
Fahad: For a long time.	*Fahad: mundhu zaman ṭawīl.*	فَهْد: مُنْذ زَمَن طَوِيْل.
Faisal: And what is this?	*Faiṣal: wamā hādhā?*	فَيصَل: وَمَا هٰذَا؟
Fahad: This is the greatest Pyramid.	*Fahad: hādhā huwa al haram al akbar.*	فَهْد: هٰذَا هُوَ الْهَرَم الأكْبَر.
Faisal: Whose Pyramid is this?	*Faiṣal: liman hādhal haram?*	فَيصَل: لِمَن هٰذَا الْهَرَم؟
Fahad: This belongs to one of the kings of Egypt. I do not remember his name.	*Fahad: limalik min mulūk miṣr. lā a'rif ismahu.*	فَهْد: لِمَلك مِن مُلُوك مِصر، لاَ أعْرِفُ اسْمَه.

Will you not take some photographs?	*Faiṣal: alā ta'khudh ba'ḍaṣ ṣuwar?*	فَيصَل: ألاَ تَاخُذ بَعْضَ الصُّوَر؟
Fahad: Why not? Sure. Stand beside the Sphinx. I'll take your photograph along with the structure. Are you ready?	*Fahad: balā, bitta'kīd. qum bi jiwari abul haul anā ākhudh ṣūratak hal anta musta'idd?*	فَهْد: بَلَى، بالتَّاكِيْد. قُمْ بِجَوارِ أبوالْهَول، أنَا آخُذ صُورَتَك، هَل أنْتَ مُسْتَعِد؟
Faisal: Yes.	*Faiṣal: na'am.*	فَيصَل: نَعَم.
Fahad: And one photograph beside the great Pyramid.	*Fahad: wa ṣūrah bi jiwāril haram al akbar.*	فَهْد: وَصُورَة بِجِوَار الْهَرَم الأكْبَر.
Faisal: The sun is about to set. We should now return to our hotel.	*Faiṣal: qarubatish shams an taghrub. linarji' al ān ilal funduq.*	فَيصل: قَرُبَت الشَّمْس أن تَغْرُب لِنَرجِع الآنَ إلَى الْفُنْدُق.

Cardinal Number

(al ‘adad al aṣlī) الْعَدَدُ الأَصْلِي

1 2 3 4 5

<u>Masculine</u>

One boy	*walad wāḥid*	وَلَد وَاحد
Two boys	*waladān ithnān*	وَلَدَان اثْنَان
Three boys	*thalāthatu aulād*	ثَلاَثَةُ أَوْلاَد
Four boys	*arba‘atu aulād*	أَرْبَعَةُ أَوْلاَد
Five boys	*khamsatu aulād*	خَمْسَةُ أَوْلاَد
Six boys	*sittatu aulād*	سِتَّةُ أَوْلاَد
Seven boys	*sab‘atu aulād*	سَبْعَةُ أَوْلاَد
Eight boys	*thamāniatu aulād*	ثَمَانِيَةُ أَوْلاَد
Nine boys	*tis‘atu aulād*	تِسْعَةُ أَوْلاَد
Ten boys	*‘asharatu aulād*	عَشَرَةُ أَوْلاَد
Eleven boys	*aḥada ‘ashara waladan*	أَحَدَ عَشَرَ وَلَداً
Twelve boys	*ithnā ‘ashara waladan*	اِثْنَا عَشَرَ وَلَداً

Thirteen boys	*thalāthata 'ashara waladan*	ثَلاَثَةَ عَشَرَ وَلَداً
Fourteen boys	*arba'ata 'ashara waladan*	أَرْبَعَةَ عَشَرَ وَلَداً
Fifteen boys	*khamsata 'ashara waladan*	خَمْسَةَ عَشَرَ وَلَداً
Sixteen boys	*Sittata 'ashara waladan*	سِتَّةَ عَشَرَ وَلَداً
Seventeen boys	*sab'ata 'ashara waladan*	سَبْعَةَ عَشَرَ وَلَداً
Eighteen boys	*thamāniyata 'ashara waladan*	ثَمَانِيَةَ عَشَرَ وَلَدا
Nineteen boys	*tis'ata 'ashara waladan*	تِسْعَةَ عَشَرَ وَلَداً
Twenty boys	*'ishrūn waladan*	عِشْرُون وَلَداً
Twenty one boys	*wāḥidun wa 'ishrūna waladan*	وَاحِدٌ وًّعِشْرُون وَلَداً
Twenty two boys	*ithnani wa 'ishrūna waladan*	اثْنَان وَعِشْرُون وَلَداً
Tweny three boys	*thalāthatun wa 'ishūuna waladan*	ثَلاَثَةٌ وَعِشْرُون ولَداً
Twenty four boys	*arba'atun wa 'ishrūna waladan*	أَرْبَعَةٌ وَعِشْرُون وَلَداً
Twenty five boys	*khamsatun wa 'ishrūna waladan*	خَمْسَةٌ وًّعِشْرُونَ وَلَداً
Twenty six boys	*sittatun wa 'ishrūna waladan*	سِتَّةٌ وَعِشْرُون وَلَداً
Thirty boys	*thalāthūna waladan*	ثَلاَثُونَ وَلَداً
Forty boys	*arba'ūna waladan*	أَرْبَعُونَ وَلَداً
Fifty boys	*khamsūna waladan*	خَمْسُونَ وَلَداً
Sixy boys	*sittūna waladan*	سِتُّونَ وَلَدا
Seveny boys	*sab'ūna waladan*	سَبْعُونَ وَلَداً
Eighty boys	*Thamānūn waladan*	ثَمَائُونَ وَلَداً

Ninety boys	*tis'ūna waladan*	تِسْعُونَ وَلَداً
One hundred boys	*mi'atu waladin*	مِائَةُ وَلَدٍ
One thousand boys	*alfu waladin*	أَلْفُ وَلَدٍ

Feminine

One girl	*bint wāḥdah*	بِنْت وَاحِدَة
Two girls	*bintan ithnatān*	بِنْتَان اثْنَتَان
Three girls	*thalāthu banāt*	ثَلاَثُ بَنَات
Four girls	*arba'u banāt*	أَرْبَعُ بَنَات
Five girls	*khamsu banāt*	خَمْسُ بَنَات
Six girls	*sittu banāt*	سِتُّ بَنَات
Seven girls	*sab'u banāt*	سَبْعُ بَنَات
Eight girls	*thamānī banāt*	ثَمَانِي بَنَات
Nine girls	*tis'u banāt*	تِسْعُ بَنَات
Ten girls	*'ashru banāt*	عَشْرُ بَنَات
Eleven girls	*iḥdā 'ashrata bintan*	إِحْدَى عَشْرَة بِنْتًا
Twelve girls	*ithnatā 'ashrata bintan*	اثْنَتَا عَشْرة بِنْتًا
Thirteen girls	*thalātha 'ashrata bintan*	ثَلاَثَ عَشْرَة بِنْتًا
Fourteen girls	*arab'a 'ashrata bintan*	أَرْبَعَ عَشْرَة بِنْتًا
Fifteen girls	*khamsa 'ashrata bintan*	خَمْسَ عَشْرَة بِنْتًا
Sixteen girls	*sitta 'ashrata bintan*	سِتَّ عَشْرَة بِنْتًا
Seventeen girls	*sab'a 'ashrata bintan*	سَبْعَ عَشْرَة بِنْتًا
Eighteen girls	*thamāni 'ashrata bintan*	ثَمَانِي عَشْرَة بِنْتًا
Nineteen girls	*tis'a 'ashrata bintan*	تِسْعَ عَشْرَة بِنْتًا

Twenty girls	*'ishrūna bintan*	عِشْرُون بِنْتًا
Twenty one girls	*iḥdawn wa 'ishrūna bintan*	إِحْدَى وَعِشْرُون بِنْتًا
Twenty two girls	*ithnatawn wa 'ishrūna bintan*	اِثْنَتَان وَعِشْرُون بِنْتًا
Twenty three girls	*thalāthun wa 'ishrūna bintan*	ثَلَاثٌ وعِشْرُون بِنْتًا
Twenty four girls	*arba'un wa 'ishrūna bintan*	أَرْبَعٌ وَعِشْرُون بِنْتًا
Twenty five girls	*khamsun wa 'ishrūna bintan*	خَمْسٌ وعِشْرُون بِنْتًا
Twenty six girls	*sittun wa 'ishrūna bintan*	سِتٌّ وَعِشْرُون بِنْتًا
Thirty girls	*thalāthūna bintan*	ثَلاَثُون بِنْتًا
Forty girls	*arba'ūna bintan*	أَرْبَعُون بِنْتًا
Fifty girls	*khamsūna bintan*	خَمْسُون بِنْتًا
Sixty girls	*sittūna bintan*	سِتُّون بِنْتًا
Seveny girls	*sab'ūna bintan*	سَبْعُون بِنْتًا
Eighty girls	*thamānūna bintan*	ثَمَانُون بِنْتًا
Ninety girls	*tis'ūna bintan*	تِسْعُون بِنْتًا
One hundred girls	*mi'atu bintin*	مِاْةُ بِنْتٍ
One thousand girls	*alfu bintin*	أَلْفُ بِنْتٍ

Ordinal Number

(al ‘adad al waṣfī) الْعَدَدُ الْوَصْفِي

Masculine

First boy	*al walad al awwal*	الْوَلَد الأوَّل
Second boy	*al walad ath thānī*	الوَلَدُ الثَّانِي
Third boy	*al walad ath thālith*	الوَلَد الثَّالِث
Fourth boy	*al walad ar rābi‘*	الوَلَد الرَّابِع
Fifth boy	*al walad al khāmis*	الوَلَد الْخَامِس
Sixth boy	*al walad as sādis*	الوَلَد السَّادِس
Seventh boy	*al walad as sābi‘*	الوَلَد السَّابِع
Eighth boy	*al walad ath thāmin*	الوَلَد الثَّامِن
Ninth boy	*al walad at tāsi‘*	الوَلَد التَّاسِع
Tenth boy	*al walad al ‘āshir*	الوَلَد العَاشِر
Eleventh boy	*al walad al ḥādī ‘ashara*	الوَلَد الْحَادِي عَشَر
Twelfth boy	*al walad ath thānī ‘ashara*	الوَلَد الثَّانِي عَشَر

Thirteenth boy	*al walad ath thālith 'ashara*	الوَلَد الثّالِث عَشَر
Fourteenth boy	*al walad ar rābi' 'ashara*	الوَلَد الرّابِع عَشَر
Fifteenth boy	*al walad al khāmis 'ashara*	الوَلَدُ الْخَامِس عَشَر
Twentieth boy	*al walad al 'ishrūn*	الوَلَد الْعِشْرُون
Twenty first boy	*al walad al ḥādī wal 'ishrūn*	الوَلَد الْحَادِي وَالْعِشْرُون
Twenty second boy	*al walad ath thānī wal 'ishrūn*	الوَلَد الثّانِي وَالْعِشْرُون
Twenty third boy	*al walad ath thālith wal 'ishrun*	الوَلَد الثّالِث وَالْعِشْرُون
Twenty fourth boy	*al walad ar rābi' wal 'ishrūn*	الوَلَد الرّابِع وَالْعِشْرون
Twenty fifth boy	*al walad al khāmis wal 'ishruna*	الوَلَد الْخَامِس وَالْعِشْرُون
Thirtieth boy	*al walad ath thalāthūn*	الوَلَدُ الثّلاثُون
Fortieth boy	*al walad al arba'ūn*	الوَلَدُ الأَرْبَعُون
Fiftieth boy	*al walad al khamsūn*	الوَلَدُ الْخَمْسُون
Sixtieth boy	*al walad assittūn*	الوَلَد السِّتُّون
Seventieth boy	*al walad as sab'ūn*	الوَلَد السَّبْعُون
Eightieth boy	*al walad ath thamānūn*	الوَلَدُ الثّمَانُون
Ninetieth boy	*al walad attis'ūn*	الوَلَد التِّسْعُون
Hundredth boy	*al walad al mi'ah*	الوَلَد الْمِئَة
Thousandth boy	*al walad al alf*	الوَلَد الأَلْف

Feminine

First girl	*al bint al ūla*	البِنْت الأُوْلَى
Second girl	*al bint ath thāniyah*	البِنْت الثّانِيَة
Third girl	*al bint ath thālithah*	البِنْت الثّالِثَة

Fourth girl	*al bint ar rābi'ah*	البنت الرَّابعَة
Fifth girl	*al bint al khāmisah*	البنت الْخامسَة
Sixth girl	*al bint as sādisah*	البنت السَّادسَة
Seventh girl	*al bint as sābi'ah*	البنت السَّابعَة
Eighth girl	*al bint ath thāminah*	البنت الثَّامنَة
Ninth girl	*al bint at tāsi'ah*	البنت التَّاسعَة
Tenth girl	*al bint al 'āshirah*	البنْت العَاشرَة
Eleventh girl	*al bint al ḥādiyah 'ashrah*	البنْت الْحَادِيَة عَشْرَة
Twelfth girl	*al bint ath thāniyah 'ashrah*	البنْت الثَّانِيَة عَشْرَة
Thirteenth girl	*al bint ath thālithah 'ashrah*	البنْت الثَّالِثَة عَشْرَة
Fourteenth girl	*al bint ar rābi'ah 'ashrah*	البنْت الرَّابِعَة عَشْرَة
Fifteenth girl	*al bint al khāmisah 'ashrah*	البنْت الْخَامِسَة عَشْرَة
Twentieth girl	*al bint al 'ishrūn*	البنْت العشْرُون
Twenty first girl	*al bint al ḥādiyah wal 'ishrūn*	البنْت الْحَادِيَة وَالْعِشْرُون
Twenty second girl	*al bint ath thāniyah wal 'ishrūn*	البنْت الثَّانِيَة وَالْعِشْرُون
Twenty third girl	*al bint ath thālithah wal 'ishrūn*	البنْت الثَّالِثَة وَالْعِشْرُون
Twenty fourth girl	*al bint ar rābi'ah wal 'ishrūn*	البنْت الرَّابِعَة والعِشْرُون
Twenty fifth girl	*al bint al khāmisah wal 'ishrūn*	البنْت الْخَامِسَة والعِشْرُون
Thirtieth girl	*al bint ath thalāthūn*	البنْت الثَّلاثُون
Fortieth girl	*al bint al arba'ūn*	البنْت الأربَعُون
Fiftieth girl	*al bint al khamsūn*	البنْت الْخَمْسُون
Sixtieth girl	*al bint as sittūn*	البنْت السِّتُّون

Seventieth girl	*al bint as sab'ūn*	البنْت السّبْعُون
Eightieth girl	*al bint ath thamānūn*	البنْت الثّمَانُون
Ninetieth girl	*al bint attis'ūn*	البنْت التسْعُون
Hundredth girl	*al bint al mi'ah*	البنْت الْمئَة
Thousandth girl	*al bint al alf*	البنْت الألْف

Fractions

(al kusūr) **الكُسُور**

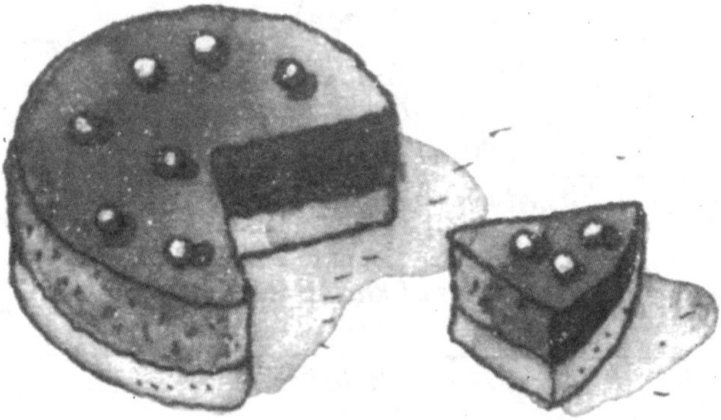

Half	*(nisf)*	نصْف
One third	*(thulth)*	ثُلْث
One fourth	*(rub')*	رُبْع
One fifth	*(khums)*	خُمْس
One sixth	*(suds)*	سُدُس
One seventh	*(sub')*	سُبْع
One eighth	*(thumn)*	ثُمْن
One ninth	*(tus')*	تسْع
One tenth	*('ushr)*	عُشْر

Months and Seasons of the Year

(shuhūr wa fuṣūlus sanah) شُهُور وفُصُول السَّنَة

Jamal: O Nasir! Do you know how many months are there in a year?	*Jamāl: yā nāṣir hal anta ta'rif kam shahran fis sanah?*	جَمَال: يَا نَاصِر هَل أَنْتَ تَعْرِف كَمْ شَهْراً فِي السَّنَــــة؟
Nasir: Yes, there are twelve months in a year.	*Nāṣir: na'am ithnā 'ashara shahran fis sanah.*	نَاصِر: نَعَم، اِثْنَا عَشَر شَهْراً فِي السَّنَة
Jamal: Do you remember their names?	*Jamāl: hal tadhkur asmā'ahā?*	جَمَال: هَلْ تَذْكُر أَسْمَاءَهَا؟
Nasir: Yes, they are:	*Nāṣir: na'am, wa hiya:*	نَاصِر: نَعَم، وَهِي:

(1) January	*(yanāyar)*	(١) يَنَايَر
(2) February	*(fabrāyar)*	(٢) فَبْرَايَر
(3) March	*(mārs)*	(٣) مَارس
(4) April	*(abrīl)*	(٤) أَبْرِيل
(5) May	*(māyu)*	(٥) مَايُو
		(٦) يُونِيُو

(6) June	*(yuniyu)*	(٧) يُولِيُو
(7) July	*(yuliyu)*	(٨) أُغُسْطُس
(8) August	*(ughusṭus)*	(٩) سِبْتَمْبَر
(9) September	*(sibtimbar)*	(١٠) أَكْتُوبَر
(10) October	*(aktūbar)*	(١١) نُوفِمْبَر
(11) November	*(nofimbar)*	(١٢) دِيْسِمْبَر
(12) December	*(dīsimbar)*	
Jamal: Good! My brother.	*Jamāl: aḥsanta yā akh.*	جَمَال: أَحْسَنْتَ يَا أَخ.
Which is the first month of the year?	*wa mā huwa awwalu shahris sanah?*	وَمَا هُوَ أَوَّلُ شَهْرِ السَّنَة؟
Nasir: It is Januray.	*Nāṣir: huwa yanāyar.*	نَاصِر: هُوَ يَنَايَر.
Jamal: And which is the last month?	*Jamāl: wa mā ākhiruhā?*	جَمَال: وَمَا آخِرُهَا؟
Nasir: It is December.	*Nāṣir: huwa dīsimbar.*	نَاصِر: هُوَ دِيْسِمْبَر.
Jamal: How many seasons are there in a year?	*Jamāl: wa kam faslan fis sanah?*	جَمَال وَكَم فَصْلاً فِي السَّنَة؟
Nasir: There are four seasons in a year. They are:	*Nāṣir: hunāk arab'atu fuṣūl fis sanah. wa hiya:*	نَاصِر: هُنَاك أَرْبَعَة فُصُول فِي السَّنَة. وَهِي:
Summer	*(aṣ ṣaif)*	الصَّيْف
Winter	*(ash shitā')*	الشِّتَاء
Spring	*(ar rabī')*	الرَّبِيْع
Autumn	*(al kharīf)*	الْخَرِيْف
Jamal: You are an intelligent boy. Which season do you like most, my brother?	*Jamāl: anta walad dhakiyy ayy faṣl aḥabbu ilaik yā akh?*	جَمَال: أَنْتَ وَلَد ذَكِيّ. أيّ فَصْل أَحَبُّ إِلَيْك يَا أَخ؟
Nasir: I like the Spring most.	*Nāṣir: aḥabbul fuṣūl ilayya huwa ar rabī'.*	نَاصِر: أَحَبُّ الْفُصُول إِلَيّ هُوَ الرَّبِيْع

In this season the weather is moderate.	*fī hādhal faṣl al jaww mu'tadil.*	فِي هَذَا الْفَصْل الْجَوّ مُعْتَدِل.
And what do you prefer, sir?	*wa mā tufaḍḍiluhu yā sayyidī?*	وما تفضله يا سيدي؟
Jamal: The spring of course.	*Jamāl: faṣlar rabī' tab'an.*	جَمَال: فَصْل الرَّبِيْع طَبْعًا.
Jamal: And how is the weather in the month of February in your country, my brother?	*Jamāl: wa kaifal jaww fī shahri fabrāyar fī baladikum yā akh?*	جَمَال: وَكَيْفَ الْجَوّ فِي شَهْرِ فَبْرَايِر فِي بَلدكُم يَا أخ؟
Nasir: The weather in this month is very pleasant.	*Nāṣir: aljawwu fī hādhas shahr laṭīfun jidda.*	نَاصِر: الْجَوُّ فِي هَذَا الشَّهْرِ لَطِيْفٌ جِدًّا.
Jamal: In which month your schoold is closed?	*Jamāl: fī ayyi shahr tughlaq madrasatuk?*	جَمَال: فِي أيّ شَهْر تُغْلَق مَدْرَسَتُك؟
Nasir: In the month of December.	*Nāṣir: fī shahri dīsimbar.*	نَاصِر: فِي شَهْر دِيْسَمْبَر
Jamal: And when does it reopen?	*Jamāl: wa matā tuftaḥ marrah ukhrā?*	جَمَال: وَمَتَى تُفْتَح مَرَّة أخْرَى؟
Nasir: In the end of January.	*Nāṣir: fī awākhiri shahri yanāyar.*	نَاصِر: فِي أوَاخِر شَهْر يَنَاير.
Jamal: When does your annual exams begin this year?	*Jamāl: wa matā yabda' ikhtibārukas sanawī fī hādhihis sanah?*	جَمَال: وَمَتَى يَبْدأ اخْتِبَارَك السَّنَوِي فِي هَذِه السَّنَة؟
Nasir: At the beginning of April.	*Nāṣir: fī awā'ili shahri abrīl.*	نَاصِر: فِي أوَائِل شَهْر أبْرِيْل.

Days and Timing

(al ayyām wat tauqīt) الأَيَّامُ وَالتَّوْقِيْت

Teacher: Do you know how many days are there in a week?	*al mu'allim: hal ta'rif kam yauman fil 'usbū'.*	الْمُعَلِّم: هَلْ تَعْرِف كَم يَوماً فِي الأسْبُوع؟
Student: Yes sir, there are seven days in a week.	*aṭṭālib: na'am yā ustādhī sab'atu ayyām fil usbū'.*	الطَّالِب: نَعَم يَا أُسْتَاذِي، سَبْعَة أَيَّام فِي الأسْبُوع.
Teacher: What are they?	*al mu'allim: wa mā hiya?*	الْمُعَلِّم: وَمَا هِي؟
Student: They are:	*aṭṭālib: hiya:*	الطَّالِب: هِي:

Sunday	*(yaumul aḥad)*	يَوْمُ الأَحَد
Monday	*(yaumul ithnain)*	يَوْمُ الاثْنَيْن
Tuesday	*(yaumuth thulāthā')*	يَوْمُ الثُّلاثَاء
Wednesday	*(yaumul arbi'ā')*	يَوْمُ الأَرْبِعَاء
Thursday	*(yaumul khamīs)*	يَوْمُ الْخَمِيْس
Friday	*(yaumul jumu'ah)*	يَوْمُ الْجُمُعَة
Saturday	*(yaumus sabt)*	يَوْمُ السَّبْت

Teacher: what do you do on Sunday?	*al mu'allim: mādhā taf'al yaumal aḥad?*	الْمُعَلِّم: مَاذَا تَفْعَل يَوْمَ الأحَد؟
Student: I go out with my parents for picnic.	*aṭṭālib: akhruj ma'a walidayya linnuzhah.*	الطَّالب: أخْرُج مَعَ وَالِدَىّ للنُّزْهَة.
Teacher: Where do you go?	*al mu'allim: ilā aina takhruj?*	الْمُعَلِّم: إلَى أيْنَ تَخْرُج؟
Student: Sometimes we go to one of the parks of the city but mostly we go out to the beach.	*aṭṭālib: nakhruj ba'ḍal aḥyān ilā ḥadīqatin min ḥadā'iqil madīnah walākin fi aktharil aḥyān nakhruj ilā shāṭi'il baḥr.*	الطَّالب: نَخْرُج بَعْضَ الأحْيَان إلَى حَدِيْقَة من حَدَائق الْمَدِيْنَة وَلَكِن فِي أكْثَرِ الأحْيَان نَخْرُج إلَى شَاطِئ الْبَحْر.
And sometimes we visit some of the relatives.	*wa ba'ḍal aḥyān nakhruj liziyārati ba'ḍil aqārib*	وَبَعْضَ الأحْيَان نَخْرُج لِزِيَارَة بَعْضِ الأقَارِب
Teacher: where did you go last Sunday?	*al mu'allim: aina dhahabta fī yaumil aḥad as sābiq?*	الْمُعَلِّم: أيْنَ ذَهَبْت فِي يَومِ الأحَد السَّابِق؟
Student: To the park.	*aṭṭālib: ilal ḥadīqah.*	الطَّالب: إلَى الْحَدِيْقَة.
Teacher: How did you find the park on that day?	*al mu'allim: kaifa wajadtal ḥadīqah fī dhālikal yaum?*	الْمُعَلِّم: كَيْف وَجَدْتَ الْحَدِيْقَة فِي ذَلِك الْيَوم؟
Student: I found it full of people.	*aṭṭālib: wajattuhā malī'atam bin nās.*	الطَّالب: وَجَدتُهَا مَلِيْئَةً بِالنَّاس.
Teacher: And what do you do on weekdays?	*al mu'allim: wa mādhā taf'al fil ayyām al ukhrā?*	الْمُعَلِّم: وَمَاذَا تَفْعَل فِي الأيَّامِ الأُخْرَى؟
Student: I attend the school punctually every day.	*aṭṭālib: aḥḍur ilal madrasah kulla yaum bil muwāẓabah.*	الطَّالب: أحْضُر إلَى الْمَدْرَسَة كُلَّ يَوم بِالْمُوَاظَبَة.
Teacher: On which day do you revise your lessons?	*al mu'allim: fī ayy yaum turāji' durūsak?*	الْمُعَلِّم: فِي أيِّ يَوْم تُرَاجِع دُرُوسَك؟
Student: I revise my lessons on Saturday.	*aṭ ṭālib: 'urāji'u durūsī yaumas sabt.*	الطَّالب: أُرَاجِع دُرُوسِي يَومَ السَّبْتِ.

Jamal: What time is it now?	*Jamāl: kamis sā'ah alān?*	جَمَال: كَم السَّاعَة الآن؟
Nasir: It's half past ten now.	*Nāṣir: as sā'ah al 'āshirah wan niṣf alān.*	نَاصر: السَّاعة الْعَاشِرة وَالنِّصْف الآن.
Jamal: When do you wake up?	*Jamāl: matā tastaiqiẓ?*	جَمَال: مَتَى تَسْتَيْقِظ؟
Nasir: I wake up at six o'clock.	*Nāṣir: astaiqiẓu fis sā'ah as sādisah.*	نَاصر: اسْتَيْقَظ فِي السَّاعَة السَّادسَة.
Jamal: When do you take your breakfast?	*Jamāl: wa matā tanāwalul fuṭūr?*	جَمَال: وَمَتَى تَنَاوَلُ الْفُطُور؟
Nasir: I take my breakfast at seven o'clock.	*Nāṣir: atanāwalul fuṭūr fis sā'ah as sābi'ah.*	نَاصر: أتَنَاوَل الْفُطُور فِي السَّاعَة السَّابعَة.
Jamal: At what time do you leave for your office?	*Jamāl: wa fī ayy sā'ah takhruj ilā maktabik?*	جَمَال: وَفِي أيِّ سَاعَة تَخْرُج إلَى مَكْتَبِك؟
Nasir: I leave at nine in the morning and reach my office at half past nine.	*Nāṣir: akhruj fis sā'ah at tāsi'ah fiṣ ṣabāḥ wa aṣilu ilaih fittāsi'ah wan niṣf.*	نَاصر: أخْرُج فِي السَّاعَة التَّاسعَة فِي الصَّبَاح وَأصل إلَيْه فِي التَّاسعَة وَالنِّصْف.
My office is very near to my house. It takes only half an hour.	*maktabi qarīb jiddā min baitī hādhā yukallifunī niṣf sā'ah faqaṭ.*	مَكْتَبِي قَرِيْب جدًا من بَيْتي، هَذَا يُكَلِّفُنِي نِصفَ سَاعَة فَقط.
Jamal: What time do you retrun from work?	*Jamāl: wa fī ayy waqt tarji' minal 'amal?*	جَمَال: وَفِي أيِّ وَقْت تَرْجِعُ مِنَ الْعَمَل؟
Nasir: I leave my office at half past five and by six I am back home.	*Nāṣir: akhruj min maktabī fis sā'ah al khāmisah wan niṣf wa aṣilu ilal bait fis sā'ah as sādisah.*	نَاصر: أخْرُج منْ مَكْتَبِي فِي السَّاعَة الْخَامسَة وَالنِّصْف وَأصل إلَى الْبَيْت فِي السَّاعَة السَّادسَة.
Five minutes past ten	*as sā'ah al 'āshirah wa khamsu daqā'iq.*	السَّاعَةُ الْعَاشِرَة وَخَمْس دَقَائق
Five minutes to six	*as sā'ah as sādisah illā khams daqā'iq*	السَّاعَة السَّادسَة إلا خَمْس دَقَائق

Quarter past four	*as sā'ah ar rābi'ah war rub'*	السَّاعَة الرَّابِعَة وَالرُّبْع
Quarter to four	*as sā'ah ar rābi'ah illar rub'*	السَّاعَة الرَّابِعَة إلاّ الرُّبْع
Twenty minutes past three	*as sā'ah ath thālithah wa 'ishrūna daqīqah.*	السَّاعَةُ الثَّالِثَة وَعِشْرُون دَقِيقَة
Ten minutes to two	*as sā'ah ath thāniyah illā 'ashrata daqā'iq.*	السَّاعَة الثَّانِيَة إلاّ عَشْرة دَقَائِق.